IN ANOTHER
LANGUAGE

IN ANOTHER LANGUAGE

A Record of the Thirty-Year Relationship between
Thomas Mann and His English Translator,
Helen Tracy Lowe-Porter

BY

John C. Thirlwall , *1904*

New York · ALFRED A. KNOPF

1966

Library of Congress Catalog Card Number: 66–12394

THIS IS A BORZOI BOOK
PUBLISHED BY ALFRED A. KNOPF, INC.

© Copyright 1966 by John C. Thirlwall. All rights reserved under International and Pan-American Copyright Conventions. Distributed by Random House, Inc. Published simultaneously in Toronto, Canada, by Random House of Canada Limited. Manufactured in the United States of America.

FIRST EDITION

Portions of the essay "On Translating Thomas Mann" by Mrs. Helen Tracy Lowe-Porter appeared in *Symposium*, Fall 1955. © Copyright 1955 by the Department of Romance Languages, Syracuse University.

PREFACE

WHEN Helen Lowe died on April 27, 1963, at the age of
eighty-six, many of the readers of Thomas Mann in
English were surprised to discover that the enigmatic
signature H. T. Lowe-Porter was that of a woman—a
small-town American woman at that. Mrs. Lowe, born
Helen Tracy Porter in the village of Towanda in northeastern Pennsylvania, where her father ran the local
drugstore, was a graduate of a small girls' college—Wells,
in Aurora, New York [1]—and would seem to be an unlikely
choice to translate the works of Thomas Mann, that
profoundly German thinker. When, however, Mrs. Lowe
came to the translation of *Buddenbrooks* in 1923, she had
a strong background in translating from French, Italian,
and Latin as well as German. She had lived abroad for
many years: in Rome, which she knew well enough to
serve as a guide for the students at the American College
of Classical Studies; in Munich, where she met Elias Avery

---

[1] In 1964 Wells College set up an annual award for superior translating
in the name of Helen Porter Lowe.

v

Lowe, whom she married in 1911; and in Oxford, where Dr. Lowe taught paleography. She had done her first translations for *Poet Lore*, edited in Boston by her blue-stocking aunt, Charlotte Endymion Porter, who introduced many European writers to America. Starting at the turn of the century with Sudermann and Hauptmann, Mrs. Lowe was to translate from Werfel, Feuchtwanger, Bruno Frank, Hermann Broch, and Albert Einstein. But her thirty-year relationship with Thomas Mann, with whom her name became as closely united as Carlyle's was with Goethe, Constance Garnett's with Dostoevski, or Scott Moncrieff's with Proust, was the backbone of her life's work. Without her translations, the name of Thomas Mann might well be as little known to the English-speaking world as that of his brother Heinrich.

In 1906 Helen Porter went to Munich to study drama, met the young and brilliant paleographer Elias Lowe, and added Latin to her stock of languages so as to help him with his doctoral dissertation. After a year she returned to Towanda, whither Dr. Lowe followed her. When he received a Carnegie Research Fellowship of $1,200, they were married in Berne in 1911 and traveled happily to Rome, where Dr. Lowe commenced his monumental *Codices Latini Antiquiores*, upon which he is still at work. In 1914 Dr. Lowe was appointed University Lecturer and Reader at Oxford. Just outside the city, the Lowes took over a rambling, comfortable old house, which was modernized and became the happy home of three growing daughters and a host of friends, English, American, and European.

What was Helen Tracy Lowe-Porter (to give her full professional name) like as a human being? Few besides

Dr. Lowe knew her at the start of this century. "There was something saintly about her," he said to me in 1964. "She never cheated and preferred even to be cheated. I never knew anyone more modest about herself and more scrupulous against doing injustice to others. Spiritual beauty shone from her countenance. Our married life had a wonderful quality which made one of our neighbors declare: 'I never knew such ideal companionship existed.'"

He was tremendously impressed by her piercing blue eyes, shining out of a rather rugged face. These eyes were the first feature that distinguished her, and not only on first acquaintance—they were never forgotten. Ida Herz, mutual friend of Thomas Mann and Helen Lowe, wrote: "I liked her from the very first minute I saw her. I was immediately fascinated by her beautiful eyes, their sparkling blue—I loved her eyes always, and if I think of her, I always see her eyes, her speaking, smiling eyes, full of expression, of kindness, of humor and good-natured mockery."

These sparkling blue eyes were not always complacent. Her second daughter, Bice, Mrs. James Fawcett, wrote:

She had bright blue eyes which when she was angry seemed to spin round like Catherine Wheels and shoot off sparks. Her anger was frightening and compelling, I think, because a complete moral integrity lay behind it. She had a passionate regard for goodness and truth; it was a fire that at times could wither weaker mortals; she did her gentle but relentless best to communicate her standards to us—a strenuous process at the time, but I think it was worth it. She did not indulge in physical demonstrations of affection, though she was the reverse of cold; she mistrusted emotional display and kept the fires banked down. In fact, she mistrusted the emotions altogether, felt that they confused things, and she had a rather impractical faith in the power of reason. All this makes her sound nothing but serious; however, she could be gay and funny and she had a particularly beautiful smile.

All three daughters and Dr. Lowe commented upon the long walking tours, sometimes averaging twenty miles a day. They walked in the Bavarian mountainside and through the Cotswolds and the Berkshire Downs, where her ashes are scattered. On these tours Mrs. Lowe would recite from memory endless passages from Shakespeare, Mark Twain, and Lewis Carroll, or from more recent poems. Her youngest daughter, Patsy, Mrs. Merlyn Pitzele, said:

She was not an aggressive person, she was shy and even retiring, save through the power of her convictions, which were forceful, but she was not one to be intimidated either. She translated the work of the Italian Himalayan explorer, Filippo di Filippi, a fiery noisy little man like a bull terrier, who terrified me, but who took enormous pleasure in my mother's company and liked the fact that she stood up to him and wasn't taken in for a minute by his bark.

My mother influenced us all very much because of the New England principles by which she herself had been brought up —austerity as to material matters, simplicity of living, rectitude, a sense of what excellence meant (both our parents were perfectionists). But she passed on to us other things as well— her love of good food and cooking, of good books and talk, her eye for color, for the exact word, for Shakespeare, Mark Twain, the Bible—these she loved.

When Mrs. Lowe was asked for some verses to go with a bust of her modeled by Gina Plunguian in 1950, she wrote:

> *A face is a face is a face:*
> *A mouth and a nose and an eye*
> *Or two, in the usual place*
> *Make us all look alike, you'll agree,*
> *So how can you tell it is me,*
> *When we're all so alike in the face?*
>
> *I boast no unusual feature,*
> *No arrangement distinctive or odd,*
> *And yet this quite commonplace creature*
> *When modelled by Gina you'll see*
> *Can surely be no one but me,*
> *Expressive in every feature.*

No classical beauty, Helen possessed a native dignity to which she added an air of open-handed friendliness—a friendliness which spread from her acquaintances to human causes: she was a passionate lover of the human race, in the line of the radical abolitionists before the American Civil War.

"As a child I saw already that she was beautiful, strong and clear-minded, with an ardent, sometimes frightening, idealism," her oldest daughter, Prue (Mrs. Prudence Smedts), wrote. "She was energetic, both in her literary work [Mrs. Lowe would get in a good eight-hour day translating] and, in the good American tradition, domestically and physically." In Maggie Tulliver of *The Mill on the Floss*, Prue found "an illumination of my mother's character." Indeed, was not Maggie's life a series of conflicts with respectability, with the normal pattern? Helen's first revolt against the norm was her marriage to a Jew, a rather unconventional choice for a girl with Helen's Protestant upbringing.

She was constantly on the side of the underdog. When Edward VIII, then Prince of Wales, espoused the cause of the striking Welsh miners, Mrs. Lowe was up in arms in his defense, and he became the hero of her play *Abdication*. One Christmas she induced the members of her family to give the money saved for presents to the miners out of work in the Rhondda Valley. "One could not but respect the 'do-good' qualities this exemplified," her daughter Patsy said, "for they were not obtrusive, merely constant. At Christmas, for example, when we were growing up in North Oxford, we would take food and present-filled stockings to the 'poor' and even sing carols to them."

It was her passionate concern for justice and mercy that led her to take a radical stand on social and political matters, a concern that drew her closer to Thomas Mann when he experienced the Nazi blast.

I met Helen Lowe in the summer of 1936, when she had turned sixty, on an Intourist bus in Leningrad. Actually we met over a bug, presented dramatically to the manager of the Hotel Astoria by an irate and unreasonable female American tourist. On the bus, we (she was traveling with Mrs. Katharine Wells, a relative of H. G. Wells) exchanged comments about how tourists can present a false picture of their own country. Finally I connected this Mrs. Lowe with H. T. Lowe-Porter and stammered my gratitude for the work she had done on Thomas Mann. When she learned that I was a college teacher who had actually read Mann, Proust, and Joyce, she adopted me as a literary son with whom she might talk on equal terms. She inscribed a copy of *Abdication* to me in these terms: "To one of my devoted admirers—with reciprocal respect." We roamed the streets of Leningrad, talking about literary and—inevitable in Russia—political matters. Mrs. Lowe was deeply sympathetic toward the Soviet revolution, but she was in Russia to decide from the facts. One day we came upon a female Phys-Kultur exercise on the promenade before the Winter Palace. As the girls strutted past, Mrs. Wells raised her arm in an enthusiastic clenched-fist salute, which Mrs. Lowe and I imitated halfheartedly. Considerable doubt of the Soviet wave of the future remained in our minds. "The Russian experience was very stirring," she wrote to Alfred A. Knopf upon her return. "There if anywhere—as an American scientist remarked to me—is some hope for the human race. Not that there is not plenty of hope elsewhere too, if we will only climb onto the bandwagon in time."

In her sixtieth year Helen Lowe was somewhat short, erect, and graceful. Her piercing blue eyes transfixed me as they had Dr. Lowe thirty years before. Whether she was fresh or exhausted from the promenades on the Nevsky Prospekt, her personal charm and tact never flagged. The three of us proceeded to Moscow, where at parties at the American Embassy, at Walter Duranty's, and at our second-class hotel I constantly admired her sang-froid and her incisive questions and answers couched in that inescapable northeastern Pennsylvania accent.

When in 1937 she followed Dr. Lowe to Princeton, New Jersey, where he was elected one of the first faculty members of the Institute for Advanced Study, our friendship was cemented. The Spanish Civil War was in full explosion, and because the Loyalists were backed only by the Soviet Union, many liberals, including Mrs. Lowe, moved further to the left in politics. There were times when Helen's anti-Fascist, pro-Communist diatribes could bore if not embarrass the company. But I early learned the trick of drawing her off in another direction by inquiring about her current work on Mann (she was then translating *Joseph in Egypt*). The more the world situation worsened under the aggressions of Mussolini and Hitler, the more she turned for solace to the difficult, almost impossible, translation of *Joseph*.

I had one small experience of Mrs. Lowe's skill as a translator of German. In the summer of 1938, shortly after the Austrian *Anschluss,* I had done slight favors for a true Nazi, Herbert Bang, and for a proscribed anti-Nazi Austrian, Dr. Victor Altmann. The Nazi had done his best to convert me to the blessings of National Socialism as we traveled through the Balkans, but I left no doubt in his mind as to my detestation of Fascism. Because he had sworn *Blut Bruderschaft* with me (for taking care of him when he was drunk), he continued by correspondence to show me the light. When Dr. Altmann, the Viennese refugee, arrived in New York, I had him and Mrs. Lowe to dinner. That day one of Herr Bang's endless letters had arrived, which I produced for translation. Dr. Altmann read sentence by everlasting sentence, and Mrs. Lowe translated without a pause. *"Nicht Stil, nicht Stil!"* Dr. Altmann muttered, but Mrs. Lowe turned this absurd propaganda into excellent English.

Mrs. Judith Bernays Heller, the Viennese-born, American-educated translator of the German letters in this book, met Helen Lowe in 1916 at Camden, North Carolina, whither Mrs. Lowe had taken her daughter Prue for treatment of asthma. "What was it that was attractive to me in Helen," Mrs. Heller remarked in 1963, "her gentleness, her kindness to me, to the children, her patience and industry, sitting down daily to her stint of translating, her bookishness, her fascinating way of telling stories of her life in Munich, her years in Rome? For me, it was primarily her simplicity, her naturalness, her interest in the people around her, the fact that she knew German and knew something of the background which had been that of my parents in Europe. We became close friends in the three weeks that I stayed with her."

Helen Lowe was a woman of many and varied interests: she was well read in several languages; she wrote poetry, plays, novels, political articles, and letters by the hundreds. Literature meant much to her, but she did not neglect the simpler household tasks, for she enjoyed cooking. On her beloved Isle au Haut, off the coast of Maine, she might be baking bread while listening to Beethoven's piano sonata in C minor, Opus 111, in preparation for her translation of Mann's *Doctor Faustus*. In music and painting she was rather weak: literature and people were her passions. Basically shy and unsure of herself, she had an abiding interest in other people and could easily strike up a conversation with strangers on a train. Her predominant interests were literature and politics—it would be hard to decide which was more important to her. In an author's questionnaire she listed her "Favorite Form of Recreation" as "Conversation," her "Hobby" as "Cooking." Under "Well-known Relatives—Ancestors" she listed "Charlotte Endymion Porter, editor of First Folio edition of Shakespeare, and of magazine *Poet Lore* (Boston)" and "Endymion Porter, seventeenth-century Englishman, courtier and poet—patron of the drama." This radical socialistic leveler felt quiet pride in her English ancestry. England and the English she loved dearly. Her family roots had been in New England; long

xiii

residence in Oxford and London, reinforced by walking tours with her children and friends in the Lake Country, strengthened these transatlantic roots. During World War II she had little sympathy for what she considered the imperialist governments of England and France, but England itself she loved devotedly. "If only by some magic we could tow lovely England to some sequestered spot on the globe, to rest free from bombs," she said to me in 1940, "the world would be better off, and I'd be happy."

She had been nurtured, after all, on the King James version of the Bible; she had been reading Shakespeare, especially the Chronicle Plays, from childhood. England, both literarily and geographically, became a passion. At the height of the Battle of Britain, when bombs were raining on London, Coventry, Southampton—almost everywhere save on Oxford—she wrote her "Litany," in invocation to the beloved towns and villages of England:

> *WORDS are dear,*
> *And names are dear.*
> *And words of place fall sweet upon the air.*
> *But most of all the names of English places,*
> *Of English settlements in English shires,*
> *Stealing like drowsy music on the ears.*
> *And specially of all the shires there be*
> *In Oxford, Bucks and Berks*
> *The names are dear to me.*

> *As:*
> *Appleford, Cottisford, Burford and Shillingford,*
> *Fairford and Frilford, Twyford and Widford:*
> *Aylesbury, Adderbury, Ashbury, Banbury,*

xiv

Bibury, Blewsbury, Charlbury, Idbury,
Binsey and Botley and Witney and Thame.
Osney Mead, Pixey Mead,
Goosey and Froggledown,
Hids Copse and Toot Baldon,
Peppard and Sparsholt,
Much Wenlock and Wantage,
Horton cum Studley
  and
Ascombe sub Edge.

O Windrush, Evenlode and Dorne,
O Bablock Hythe and Great and Little Tew,
Pray for us, we pray for you!

Then:
Loudwater, Highclere, Shiplake and Swallowfield,
Wendover, Shotover, Wychwood and Elsfield,
Farnborough, Hanborough, Longborough, Risborough,
Cricklade and Lechlade, Ewelme and Yarnton,
Besselsleigh, Nettlebed, Ilsley and Coln.
Oakhanger, Savernake,
Sonning and Sunningwell,
Enstone and Ibstone,
Wood Eaton and Water,
Long Compton and Fenny,
Chalfont Saint Giles
  and
Stanton Saint John.

O Lucknor, Charlton, Waterperry,
O Cuckhamsley and Great and Little Tew,
Pray for us, we pray for you!

So:
Abingdon, Ashendon, Bullingdon, Cassington,
Ipsden and Cuddesdon, Faringdon, Garsington,
Kidlington, Missenden, Oddington, Uffington,
Watlington, Yattendon, Wittenham, Shrivenham,
Nuneham and Amersham, Wytham and Tring.
Aston Tirrold, Letcombe Basset,
Minster Lovel, Kingston Lisle,
Rotherford Greys and Rotherford Prior,
Berwick Salome and Littlewick Green.
Moreton-in-the-Marsh and Bourton-on-the-Water,
Stanford-in-the-Vale
        and
Stow-on-the-Wold.

O Godstow, Winterbourne and Christmas Common,
O Summerfield and Great and Little Tew—
O more sweet syllables than I can summon,
Pray, pray, oh pray for us, we pray for you!

While living in Princeton, she became a close friend of Albert Einstein, whose papers and addresses she translated. He had a warm affection and strong admiration for her—*ein prachtvoller Mensch,* he called her. She could mingle easily with one of the world's great like Gilbert Murray, but she also could and did mingle easily with simple people like the caretaker on Isle au Haut. It was her ability to live on the heights of literary excellence and to mingle with the crowd that gave her an extraordinary insight into the works of the men she translated. With Mann in particular she shared a *Lebensauffassung*—an outlook on life. Their outlooks on life had not always coincided. For half his life Mann was not in any sense a "political animal." His first foray into politics was *Betrachtungen eines Unpolitischen* (1918), his conservative exchange with his more liberal brother, Heinrich; later he refused to permit its translation. Mrs. Lowe urged him several times to let her work on it, but he refused. "I am not really a literary bird," she explained. "T. Mann says that I am a sociological, not a literary bird." This sociological-avian side found wings in her play *Abdication*.

Their relationship went beyond the political. "Mann appreciated Helen's intellectual capacity," Ida Herz wrote. "He enjoyed her wit, her easy, mocking humor, the dryness of her common sense." Miss Herz thinks, however, that "Dr. Lowe is wrong when he suggests that Mann was 'somewhat jealous of her intellectual abilities.' If Dr. Lowe understands 'intellectual abilities' to mean a talent for quick, thrusting argument, relying purely on reason and intellect, then Mann had no 'intellectual ambitions.' At times he admired the quick wit of his wife and his two oldest children, Erika and Klaus, the great intellectual power of his brother, Heinrich. But he did not aspire to them for himself, and, in fact, did not rate them very high, for he found them an obstacle to creativeness."

For her part, Mrs. Lowe tried always to translate like an alter ego of the author, independent in thought and feeling though she was. Over their thirty years of association, much of Mann was bound to rub off on Mrs. Lowe; certainly his mytho-magic preoccupation in the *Joseph* series did. When Mrs. Lowe was interviewed on her seventy-fourth birthday, she told the interviewers that three and its multipliers had been of great importance to her—that she could compose verses of three, six, or nine lines with the greatest of ease. A psychologist had explained this facility in terms of her life, in which every significant happening occurred in threes: she had lived in three houses, nine years in each; she had three daughters —but only one husband. "Only one," she replied, "but Elias is as good as three."

For the relationship between Mann and his favored English translator, who rendered into an idiom acceptable in both England and America almost everything that Mann wrote, from *Buddenbrooks* to *The Holy Sinner*, I have depended upon 140 letters written to her by Thomas Mann [2] from 1924 to 1955, the year of his death, and 32 letters to her from Katia Mann. I used those letters of Mrs. Lowe which survive, her articles "On Translating Thomas Mann" [3] and "Doctor Faustus" (unpublished); also comments spoken or written by Dr. Lowe, Katia Mann, the three Lowe daughters, and friends of Thomas Mann and Mrs. Lowe. Mrs. Judith Bernays Heller has been of the greatest assistance. Born in Vienna, the niece of Sigmund Freud, brought to the United States when she was three years old, graduated from Barnard College, she returned to Vienna to marry a Viennese doctor. The *Anschluss* between Germany and Austria forced Dr. and Mrs. Heller to emigrate to the United States in 1938. From time to time, Mrs. Heller lived with Mrs. Lowe, whom she helped with her translations. A better translator of the German letters in this book could not have been invented; furthermore,

[2] Frau Katia Mann wrote to me on July 27, 1964: "I never did know there existed so many letters to Helen, which really form nearly an autobiography, some also being highly interesting."

[3] Parts of this essay were published in *Symposium*, Syracuse University, Fall 1955, and reprinted in *Wells College Alumnae News*, January 1957.

Mrs. Heller helped to edit this tribute to Thomas Mann and Helen Lowe.

In 1957 Helen asked me to arrange the sale of the bulk of her Mann material to the Yale Library—letters, manuscripts or typescripts of articles, stories, and novels, including *Doctor Faustus, Joseph the Provider,* and *The Transposed Heads.* There were some one hundred letters from Mann, written mainly in German, but some in English, to which her daughter, Mrs. Merlyn Pitzele, added forty more found in Mrs. Lowe's effects as a gift to the Yale Library. Translated by Mrs. Heller, these are here published in full or in excerpt with the full permission of Frau Katia Mann and the Yale Library.

The question may be raised: Why are so few of Mrs. Lowe's letters to Thomas Mann included? The answer was provided by Frau Mann in Kilchberg. After calling her secretary, only to discover that none of Helen's letters remained, she explained that in 1933 they had lost everything in Nazi Munich; in their travels much had had to be jettisoned. So I have had to depend upon the few carbon copies Mrs. Lowe made of her letters to Mann and to others.

As the author of this book (more properly the redactor, as so much of it was written originally by Thomas Mann and Helen Lowe), I must express my thanks for the cordial treatment accorded me at the Sterling Library of Yale University and at the Thomas Mann Archives in Zurich. As a group, university librarians are among the most decent and kindly creatures in the world.

My thanks are due most particularly to Elias Avery Lowe, his daughters, Prue (Mrs. Prudence Smedts), Bice

(Mrs. James Fawcett), and Patsy (Mrs. Merlyn Pitzele); to Miss Helen Dukas, amanuensis of Albert Einstein; and to Miss Ida Herz, long-time friend of Thomas Mann.

J. C. T.

New York, 1965

CONTENTS

IN ANOTHER

LANGUAGE

~~~~~~~~

W hile living in Oxford and raising her three daughters, Mrs. Lowe did not want to vegetate intellectu-
ally, and so let it be known that she was available as a
translator from Italian, French, or German. She had
already done some books for the firm of William Heinemann in London when one day in 1922 she received a
copy of the German edition of *Buddenbrooks*, a runaway
success in Germany early in the century but virtually
unknown in England and America. In her interesting
article, "On Translating Thomas Mann," Mrs. Lowe recalled (1950):

To me personally *Buddenbrooks* was a welcome and delightful phenomenon, for German novelists and most German
dramatists have always been for my taste too sentimental. I
certainly preferred the *brutale* to the pronouncedly romantic.
I endorsed this backwash of the romantic movement and welcomed "emotion cooled off and served up on ice.". . . I greatly
enjoyed translating *Buddenbrooks*. Such work can give one a

large measure of the pleasures of creative authorship. I got $750 for the two volumes.

Early in 1924, Mann read parts of her *Buddenbrooks* translation, which he considered "extraordinarily sensitive and accomplished," as he wrote to her on April 11, from Munich:

How skillfully and to the point you have translated the occasional verses occurring in the book! And the difficulty which you mention in the preface concerning the impossibility of rendering the dialect has been solved by you in a manner which has banished any possible trace of disappointment on my part.[1]

What has reached me from America in the way of critical comment up to now does not sound very encouraging. There are complaints about the length of the book, this somewhat illogically, since qualities are conceded to it which would make length an advantage rather than the contrary. However, all

---

[1] In her Translator's Note, Mrs. Lowe had written: "*Buddenbrooks* was written before the turn of the century; it was first published in 1901 and became a German classic. It is one of those novels—we possess many of them in English—which are at once a work of art and the unique record of a period and a district. *Buddenbrooks* is great in its psychology, great as the monument of a vanished cultural tradition, and ultimately great by the perfection of its art: the classic purity and beautiful austerity of its style.

"The translation of a book which is a triumph of style in its own language is always a piece of effrontery. *Buddenbrooks* is so leisurely, so chiseled: the great gulf of war divides its literary method from that of our time. Besides, the author has recorded much dialect. This difficulty is insuperable. Dialect cannot be transferred.

"So the present translation is offered with humility. It was necessary to recognize that the difficulties were great. Yet it was necessary to set oneself the bold task of transferring the spirit first and the letter so far as might be; and above all, to make certain that the work of art, coming as it does to the ear, in German, like music out of the past, should, in English, at least *not* come like a translation—which is, 'God bless us, a thing of naught.'"

4

disapproval concerns me alone. What you have achieved will always earn due credit.

In this letter he suggested that he and Frau Mann might stop in Oxford, but specified no date. When they dropped in unannounced, Mrs. Lowe said, "no one was at home and the Manns waited, and I feel sure T. Mann looked over all the books in our scanty library (mostly paleographical) and did his best to size up this unknown instrument which —due to the vicissitudes of those war and postwar years— must willy-nilly (and of course unless he could find a better one) serve him to change the garment of his art into one which might clothe her for the marketplace until times changed."

Thus commenced a literary and personal relationship which was to end only with Mann's death in 1955. Of that first meeting, Mrs. Lowe recalled "an atmosphere of stiffness; of not enough common ground; of a certain unreality. I felt shy, ignorant and insecure, and painfully aware of my faulty speaking German and the poor impression I must be making." But, she added significantly, "at bottom I was arrogantly sure that I was nearly always well aware of the author's larger creative purposes."

She described Mann at the age of forty-eight as

a tallish, slenderish man of good figure, possibly slightly hollow-chested . . . thin at the temples, with a sensitive mouth and hands, blue eyes, dark skin and no traits otherwise remarkable save for a fine, bold, jutting nose. He wore a dark-blue pinstripe suit, in the correctest possible fashion, and might have been a businessman, like Hans Castorp's Uncle-Cousin James. His manner was rather dry and stiff, though kindly. . . .

5

When I read *Buddenbrooks*, I deduced its author as an elderly man with—I don't know why—a white beard. The aloof disillusionment of mood in the book seemed to me something quite different from youthful cynicism or revolt. Its inhuman detachment persuaded me that the author had arrived at it after a long life and much worldly experience. When I learned my mistake, I learned at the same time something else; that T.M. had been in his youth an editor of *Simplicissimus.* I would not suggest that he derived his sardonic, his "scurrile" (in the German sense) humour from that magazine; it is certainly native to himself, one ingredient in his complex nature. I venture to suggest that it is a product of his mixed stock (his mother was a Brazilian, his father a North German merchant, an aristocrat, and Senator of the Lübeck Senate).

The Manns' visit to Oxford occurred just five years after World War I, and many of the English dons were most reluctant to welcome a German unless he shared the "sense of guilt" which was felt to be "the proper attitude of all worthy Germans," as Mrs. Lowe put it. The Lowes did their best to soften the cold reception by the Oxford faculty. Dr. Lowe walked Mann through the venerable colleges, but could extort not one word about Oxford antiquities, not even about the High. Mann did unbend somewhat over tea with Gilbert Murray, and the Manns left feeling that they had made good friends. When, after a long trip, the Manns returned to their Munich home, he sent this letter from Munich on May 20, 1924:

Dear Mistress Lowe [*sic*]:

I should like to announce to you and to your husband our safe arrival at home and send you across the sea and the land which separates us our heartiest greetings. We had a splendid journey to Hamburg on the fine American boat the *Orbite* (15,000 tons) and from there traveled to Berlin, where all kinds of business arrangements as well as family contacts kept us for a few days.

Thanks to you and to Dr. Lowe's solicitude and guidance we are greatly tempted to consider our stay in Oxford the real culmination of our journey. It was delightful. To breathe the air of English humanistic culture, that particularly fine variety of a spirit already in its decline (as Tolstoi would have it), really was fascinating for me.

Summerlike temperatures welcomed us in Germany. Our small garden was hardly green when we left, but is now bright green, and some of the plants have already lost their blossoms. It will be good to go to work again after all our adventures.

May all be well with you and with your learned spouse, whom I see before me still in his academic dress with gown and beret. And let us thank you both most heartily for all your friendliness. We hope that we may meet again, no matter where that may be.

Your devoted
Thomas Mann

In this year *Der Zauberberg* had been published in German and Mrs. Lowe was eager to do it in English, so she asked Mann if he would not accept her as his authorized translator. On March 16, 1924, Mann replied cautiously:

I do not doubt that I shall have good cause to wish that you might translate other works of mine. However, Mr. George Scheffauer, an American residing in Germany who has translated my story "Bashan and I" ["Herr und Hund," also known in English as "A Man and His Dog"], made the same proposal to me as you did, that once and for all I might name him as

7

the authorized translator, but on the advice of my publishers I did not give him this assurance for good and all in order not to be restricted as far as the English-American publishers might be affected by this. And consequently I cannot act differently in your case. Notwithstanding, I trust that your activity as mediator between me and English readers will not be limited to a single book.

With sincere greetings,
Your very devoted,
Thomas Mann

While she was waiting for Mann to choose his translator, she asked him to recommend "German books that might lend themselves to translation into English." On August 8, he replied:

That is a real problem! The good German books of the present day are all heavy, problematic, and will scarcely be suited to Anglo-Saxon ways of thoughts. For example, I cannot imagine an English version of Alfred Döblin, really a forceful writer. An author of more European quality in the way of a lighter and democratically minded trend you will find in Bruno Frank, who has just completed a book on Frederick the Great, three moralistically viewed aspects of his life.

Mrs. Lowe did translate Bruno Frank's *Tage des Königs* as *The Days of the King* (1924), and his *Ein Mann Namens Cervantes* as *A Man Named Cervantes* (1934). In 1936 she translated a collection of eight stories by Franz Werfel as *Twilight of the World.*

For months the jockeying about who was to translate *Der Zauberberg* dragged on, even when Alfred and Blanche Knopf urged Mann to commission Helen Lowe to do it. Somehow Mann felt that a woman, even the woman who had translated *Buddenbrooks* *"wie geboren,"* could not work satisfactorily on *Der Zauberberg*. On April 25, 1925, he wrote her:

I question whether the personality of a translator perfectly fit as it was for transmitting the essence of *Buddenbrooks,* would be able to manifest its special talents equally successfully for *Der Zauberberg*. This new book is essentially different from the former one—which takes place in a bourgeois environment and has an epically realistic tone; whereas the new book with its deeply intellectual and symbolic character makes quite other demands on the translator—demands which I sometimes deem would be more readily met by a male rather than a female temperament. I do not know whether such thoughts and doubts have ever occurred to you, though, in view of your intelligence, I would consider it possible. I admit without hesitation that I have written my views to Knopf, not concealing from him at the same time how highly I prize you personally as well as how much I admire your literary skill. . . . But quite aside from all personal and human factors—speaking merely in the interest of a work which happens to be my own—I would suggest that if any scruples or doubts concerning the task happen to have occurred to you, you do not hide them from the American publisher.

Mann concluded this assertion of masculine psychological superiority with the appeal: ". . . before you definitely decide to approach the task, do take into account the extraordinary difficulties it involves and make your decision accordingly."

Mrs. Lowe did not take lying down this condescending male assumption of female inability. She sent her husband Mann's letter with her own comment written on the back:

9

I need not say to you, for you know it, I suppose, that just that *"männliche Konstitution"* which is the fibre of the book, and just those speculations on *Zeitrechnung*—relativity, and just those searching parallels between flesh and spirit, are what I should enjoy worming my way into. That does not by any means convince me that the result would be as good as Dr. Scheffauer's result, of course.

She had started this plea with a logical survey of the situation:

I received this letter this morning from Dr. Mann. Of course, before sending a reply, I should much like to get your reaction to it. No, not your reaction, for that is too immediate and wo'd therefore be likely to be the result of feeling. Instead I should like you to set yourself the problem as an objective one. Here is the author, with certain distinct ideas on the subject—that he should have mentioned them before is hardly to the point—there are the publishers, to whom he has written; there is Dr. Scheffauer, certainly as far as knowledge of literature and of German goes, superior to me; and here am I, as you know me.

Mrs. Lowe, without waiting for her husband's advice, concluded that she would write to Mann

that I will take his advice and once more propose to myself a thorough-going survey of the difficulties; that ever since reading a little way into the book I have felt a great desire to tackle exactly the difficulties he mentions; but I will be quite frank if on further examination I feel serious doubts.

Then, after she had "resigned the work with mingled feelings of pride, defeat, and relief," the work was hers. Mr. Scheffauer jumped or fell from a window, and his widow attempted to carry on his translation. But Blanche and Alfred Knopf would have nothing to do with this arrangement; it is greatly to their credit that they had the perspicuity to induce Mann to take Mrs. Lowe as translator and Mrs. Lowe to continue the work.

She hesitated. "I had great misgivings, almost amounting to an infantile fear, that after all I was not capable of understanding the author's creative purposes," she noted in "On Translating Thomas Mann,"

a fear that was not lessened by a letter from Mann himself expressing his view that though I had rendered the *Buddenbrooks* into English *"wie geboren,"* it was scarcely likely that any woman could grasp the cultural parable expressed in the symbolic technique of the novel. That letter should have stimulated me, but it did not, although in theory I was a confirmed and express proponent of what in those long-ago days was called "women's rights," and under my aunt's tutelage had read assiduously the defense of women as human beings. No—partly my pride was touched at the idea of forcing myself into a commercial bargain with an unwilling author; but partly I was scared—though on grounds not that "Woman" but this particular poor specimen was unequal to the task.

After Mann had written "a kindly letter more compounded of hope than of faith," as she put it, urging her to do the translation, he sent a copy of *Der Zauberberg* to Paris, where she started translating, although she later developed an aversion to reading German in Paris. While she was at work, she appealed from time to time for help on difficult passages, and Mann could not forbear the dig (August 9, 1926):

I am not surprised that you have encountered serious difficulties in the course of your work. You know that I took such difficulties into account before you started, and even undertook to warn you of them. However, I believe that they can be surmounted and whatever I am able to do to help you accomplish this I shall do gladly.

In principle I might say that a too free translation of Peeperkorn's abrupt manner of speech would not be welcome. I am as a matter of principle in favor of a literal and exact rendition as far as this is possible in another language, and therefore I believe that Peeperkorn's idioms and bits of speech should follow the original as closely as feasible by the use of the corresponding English words and idioms, without any transposition and editing. There must surely be turns of speech in English for the German *perfekt, absolut, erledigt* which are used with the same meaning. In order to be able to advise you for special cases I ought to have these doubtful instances at hand and I beg you to let me know what they are. The word *regieren* [rule] about which you inquire is not some customary and current boyish expression but rather the playful and childish word which young Hans Castorp uses mentally for his politico-philosophic speculations, and here too an exact and literal translation into English is properly made by the English word which corresponds in usage to our *regieren*.

In November 1926 the translation was completed, but the English title had not been selected. Mann wrote on the 16th:

I was very glad to hear from you again in person after having received from Mrs. Knopf such fine reports about the completion of the *Zauberberg* translation. Though you may wish to limit my pleasure by giving me fair warning, I do believe that the judgment of Mrs. Knopf, well read and critical as she is, may well be trusted. In any case, this voluminous task is finished and I herewith send you my heartiest congratulations.

I shall dispatch the telegram concerning the title at once tomorrow. After some thought, it seems to me that *The Magic Mountain* is the more literal and more appropriate title. For "enchanted" really means placed under a spell, which could really only be applied to the enchanted hero, but not to the mountain, which is only a magical, a "magi" mountain. Nor is there any danger, it seems to me, that the word "magic" is any less suggestive or picturesque than "enchanted."

I was interested to hear of the plan to make a new translation of "Death in Venice" [*Der Tod in Venedig*]; this surprised me somewhat and I had my doubts as to the necessity of that. For I have frequently heard from various people that the translation which appeared in *The Dial* [2] was especially good and poetical. But, of course, I cannot judge whether what you say about this American version as not being quite adequate for English readers is correct. I should prefer not to give any opinion in this matter and would leave the decision to more expert judges.

Even before he received the copies of the translation, Mann took an almost childish pleasure in the reception of his novel in England:

Please accept my hearty thanks for your kind letter of January 9, from which I received the glad confirmation of what I had already learned from Mr. Knopf, namely that the corrections on *The Magic Mountain* have been completed and that, *rebus bene gestis,* you have returned to Oxford. I may say that I look forward to the appearance of the book with great pleasure and expectation, but at the same time fully confident, for I have the happy and comforting impression that you have devoted the greatest care to the translation and that a book will be presented to the English-reading public

[2] By Kenneth Burke. Republished by Alfred A. Knopf in 1965.

which does full justice to the intentions of the original, as far as this is possible.

Your account of the meeting of Dr. Baldwin with that personality from Davos entertained me greatly. How small the world is in reality, and what purposeful meetings do occur in it! Is it possible that Mr. Baldwin told Mr. Jessen of the coming English version of the novel? It seems that the book even before its appearance is enjoying a certain kind of reputation in the English-speaking world. This is corroborated by the following confused little anecdote, which I read recently: An Englishman arriving in Davos puts this first question to the porter: "Where is the German sanatorium of Dr. Mann?" Is this not encouraging?

I thank you with all my heart for all the devoted labor with which you have handled my book and, for today, am with heartiest greetings . . .

On May 22, 1927, he wrote Mrs. Lowe:

. . . yesterday I received several copies of *The Magic Mountain* and the emotions which I felt on receiving the book in its English version urged me above all to express to you my sincere appreciation of the great and the stirring effort which you have made to give this difficult and unwieldy work its form and character for the English-reading public. Insofar as I have been able to apply myself to reading it to date—and within the limits of my knowledge of the language—it seems to me that your efforts and your faithfulness to the original have been crowned with signal success. I feel, above all, that the personality of Hans Castorp, I really mean his way of expressing himself, is rendered surprisingly well in English. And, also the difficulties presented by the figure of Peeperkorn seem to me to be mastered completely. Altogether you have known how to adapt my way of expression to the English idiom, although—as I would like to believe—certain Low German, almost Anglicized tendencies of my style may have made this part of your task easier. Slight errors of litttle importance are always unavoidable. For example, the idiom *Da könnte jeder kommen* (anybody might permit himself that), said by the councillor to Hans Castorp in the first volume, when he tells Castorp that "weeping in public is not permitted here," does not mean, as you translated it, "Somebody might come," but means "If you weep, anybody might have the right to weep." But these are matters of little moment. I was especially moved by your short note of introduction, the modesty of which is in notable contrast to the immensity of the task you have so well achieved, and no less so to the overwhelming lack of skill of certain translators. . . . Permit me therefore to send you my heartfelt thanks for your devoted effort, and to congratulate you most sincerely. I trust that the English-reading public will grant Knopf and you the same measure of gratitude.

With hearty greetings and regards to you and to your husband from my wife and myself, I am, dear Mrs. Lowe . . .

This is Mrs. Lowe's "short note of introduction":

The translator wishes to thank, in this place, a number of scholars, authorities in the various special fields entered by *The Magic Mountain,* without whose help the version in all humility here offered to English readers, lame as it is, must have been more lacking still. That they gave so generously is not to be interpreted otherwise than as a tribute to a work of genius. But with all their help, the great difficulty remained: the violet had to be cast into the crucible, the organic work of art to be remoulded in another tongue. Shelley's figure is perhaps not entirely apt here. Yet, since in the creative act word and thought are indivisible, the task was seen to be one before which artists would shrink and logical minds recoil.

In 1927 *The Magic Mountain* was published simultaneously in England and the United States; its enthusiastic reception in the United States is history. The Mann cult formed in the English-speaking world, and Mann, who had been passed over for the Nobel Prize for Literature (unfairly, he believed), was granted the coveted award in 1929.

There was no further question about his English translator. Mrs. Lowe was called upon to translate every subsequent novel except *The Black Swan* and the final *Felix Krull*.[3] Alfred Knopf, eager to keep the Borzoi Mann publications uniform, even asked her to retranslate stories already done by Herman George Scheffauer and by Kenneth Burke.

Busy as she was to be for the next twenty-five years with Mann's novels, stories, and essays and the demands of a growing family, Mrs. Lowe also found time to translate other German authors. She also poured forth an endless procession of letters, articles, poems, essays, short stories, and plays. She wrote a novel, *Sea Change* (unpublished), a highly symbolic study of an American family in Europe, strongly influenced by her association with Mann. The Mann-Lowe relationship helped both the writer and the translator, but, practically speaking, it helped Mann more than it helped Mrs. Lowe. She kept her literary agents busy with play, novel, short story, poem, and political or social essay, but she could find publishers only for the play *Abdication* (Knopf) and for her small volume *Casual Verse* (Oxford). "Once a translator, always a translator," she complained to Mann.

[3] A. Cecil Curtis earlier had translated *Königliche Hoheit* as *Royal Highness*, which Alfred A. Knopf published in 1916.

When Mann was gathering material for *Three Essays* (Knopf, 1929), he sent Mrs. Lowe this interesting but undated comment:

You expressed the wish to my wife to hear from me with regard to the essay books to be published shortly. There are three essays in question: "Frederick the Great and the Grand Coalition," "Goethe and Tolstoy," and "An Experience in the Occult."

A short description of these would be the following: The Frederick essay is the result of one of my longest studies of the subject, which I had dreamed of turning into a novel. Then the war came, and the confusion its outbreak caused resulted in the sudden and passionate passing of this concept, which might be explained by saying that the essay joins a depth of foundation with a certain liveliness of presentation.

The two other essays can be considered sequels of *The Magic Mountain* and essayistic studies. It was the problem of humanity in its connection with the concept of health and sickness which occupied my mind when writing the novel. It is this problem which relates the essay to "Goethe and Tolstoy" (the subtitle of which is "Fragments of the Problem of Humanity"). Still plainer are the connections of the essay on the occult with a chapter in *The Magic Mountain,* namely, the one which bears the title "Highly Questionable." The essay is nothing more than an almost novelistic description of a seance with the Munich occultist investigator Dr. Schrenck-Notzing, and it could easily be shown how this report—in the corresponding chapter of the novel, in detail as in the whole tone—has served me.

In a letter of February 25, 1929, Mann wrote to encourage her in her work on the essays and to warn her about his major project, the *Joseph.*

I was very glad to hear from you again and to learn that the translation of the volume of essays is under way. You sense quite correctly that those pages in the chapter "Education" in the essay "Goethe and Tolstoy" are antiquated and should be omitted in the English version. I do not know whether your feeling is that they should be merely crossed out, mechanically, or whether it would be necessary to insert a number of connecting statements in place of what has been omitted. I believe that the latter procedure will be called for, but at the moment I am hard-pressed with other literary work and would like to postpone that business for a time. How far have you progressed with the translation? Should you write me that you require the text to be substituted I will send it to you.

I can surely leave it to your tact and good taste to decide whether the first person plural is so foreign to English usage that it must be replaced by the first person singular in the English version. Actually, even in German, the *wir* [we] is meant to be somewhat playfully non-modern, and is a kind of slight, literary coquetry. If the effect of its use in English exceeds this intention, it must be taken account of in the translation.

I believe we can put off to a later day the question of the simultaneous appearance in English and German of the *Joseph.* For that book is not intended to be a novel in the accepted sense, but rather an attempt at an epic work, unfashionably long-winded, for the creation of which persistent patience is necessary. And although 400 pages of it will soon be completed, the book has not progressed far enough for me to consider at this time the technical problems of its publication. Nevertheless, I can already give you a precise opinion in this respect: I do not believe that successive translations from the manuscript are impossible, because you are already familiar with my ways and have an idea of what the book is about. . . . I am now approaching the end of the tale of Jacob's life, which is in fact the prelude, and the whole life-history of Joseph still lies ahead. I may add, however, that a work dealing with such an unusual context presents the greatest problems at its beginnings, and that progress on the second half will presumably be swifter.

The writing of the *Joseph* did go slowly, for it was not until November 1931 that Mann sent Mrs. Lowe parts of the German text "so that you may at least begin to translate them." And in January 1932 he added: "I can well understand that the piecemeal translation of the Joseph novel is both an unaccustomed and an unsatisfying task; but in the end, I would assume that you would have become familiar with the style of the book, even from those parts which you have." It was in 1934 that the translation of the first volume, *Joseph and His Brothers,* appeared in English, the next two following more rapidly, as Mann had predicted: *Young Joseph* in 1935 and *Joseph in Egypt* in 1938. *Joseph the Provider* was not to appear until 1944.

Meanwhile Mrs. Lowe had translated and Knopf had published: "Death in Venice" (1930), "Mario and the Magician" (1931), and *Past Masters and Other Papers* (1933).[4] In 1936 Knopf published, as *Stories of Three Decades,* Mrs. Lowe's translations of all of Mann's shorter fiction prior to 1940.

The quality of Mrs. Lowe's translations was widely

---

[4] At Mann's special request, she translated his *Lebensabriss* (*Die Neue Rundschau,* July 7, 1930) for a limited edition by Harrison of Paris. Knopf republished this as *A Sketch of My Life* in 1960.

recognized, seldom caviled at. Mann wrote to his son Klaus about *Joseph:* "The Lowe does her work very well, but very slowly" (*Briefe* [April 27, 1943], II, 309). Lewis Galantière, a well-known translator, called her the "queen of translators." Dorothy Thompson, herself an occasional German translator, wrote in 1935: "I know what a terrifically difficult person [Mann] is to translate—with that abstruse, complicated and heavily-laden style, and I think you have done a magnificent job [on *Joseph and His Brothers*] . . . as I read the English text I wasn't conscious of you at all, and this sort of self-effacement is the finest thing a translator can perform."

Self-effacement in a translator can be an invaluable quality, no doubt, but sometimes it can be carried too far. Mrs. Lowe had so lost herself in the Mann translations that she was considered by some as a mere Mann appendage. A female Cambridge don once wrote to Mrs. Lowe asking for her "translation of Thomas Mann's play *Abdication.*"

It might be said that Mrs. Lowe invited oblivion by the overly humble tone of her Translator's Notes to Mann's books. We may remember that in her note to *Buddenbrooks* she concluded that a translation is "God bless us, a thing of naught." Even shorter was her note to *The Magic Mountain,* which had presented veritable mountains of difficulty to the translator. To the prodigious Joseph tetralogy no note at all was appended.

This self-deprecation did not match her confident note when she indicated her determination to "worm [her] way into" the *"männliche Konstitution"* of *The Magic Mountain.* As she noted in her essay "On Translating Thomas Mann":

I cannot enter into the work of other writers unless their themes and techniques and general *Lebensauffassung* appeal to me as what I should have been employing as original work. And here, I dare say (aside from the dribble of money . . .), lies the reason why I translated at all. I had begun this curious task of marrying word-cultures rather superficially, but I think the ground was always the same: the pleasure of using words without the fatal and irrevocable responsibility of using ideas. Shameless, but to an extent true. This great artist [Mann], of a controlled mental energy and scope so great it was like nothing I had ever imagined before . . . was using my ideas and so I used him to give myself private satisfactions. What a tool! What—in short—cheek! It is true I could not wield quite all of him, even in fancy—as I have said.

We may well wonder what underlay this excessive self-deprecation, for Mann frequently sent her sections of manuscript of the novels before the German editions appeared, whereupon she would work as amanuensis and editor of the original.

Mrs. Lowe's encomium was written some time after the completion of her translation of the Joseph series, some twenty years after her "vivid memory of revising the Prelude to the first of the Joseph books while sitting up in a German pension in the autumn of 1933." Her translations appeared from 1934 to 1944, a fateful decade.

Mrs. Lowe's daughter Prue recalls the inception of the translation of the Joseph series in the unbiblical surroundings of Ticonderoga on Lake George:

The lake was frozen hard, the ice groaning and creaking, and in the night there was the sound of shunting freight cars and the forlorn but comforting whistle of the train approaching Montcalm Landing.

We sat by a handsome, black iron stove, in a warm, snow-lit room, where we could often smell a good meal in preparation. . . .

In these surroundings of total contrast to the stuff of her translations we took up the two texts and began to read: "Very deep is the well of the past . . ." and around us, tangible and enclosing with magic words, spread the rich, oil-perfumed, marble-worked, oriental world of Thomas Mann's setting of the tale of Joseph:" "Should we not call it bottomless?" Reading on, through the explorations in the Prelude of the labyrinths of myth and history, slowly we made our way into the immense story of Joseph and His Brothers.

For me this minute share in her work, in these particular circumstances, remains a precious experience. Years later, we spent some time together when working on *Doctor Faustus*, and there, among the rocks and firs of that Maine Island, I saw again her capacity for entering wholly into a new world, the deep-leaved forests of European music. Not only from what I have heard said, but from my own feeling on reading her translations, I know how perfectly and conscientiously she could rebuild a work of literature in another language.

What a weary road to follow! Mann made it a practice to inform his translators what books he was reading in preparation for his novels. The account in Genesis of Joseph and his brethren, his ancestors and enemies, was not enough for Mann. He brought in other books of the Bible, Hebrew commentaries such as the *Midrash Sepher Hayasher* and *Rashi, The Koran,* even Persian poets like Firdusi. Egyptology, Orientology, and comparative mythology and religion, to say nothing of Freudian psychology, all played their part. Valiantly, Mrs. Lowe immersed herself in background works while she was turning out the translation. "The *Joseph* is going slowly along," she wrote to Mann on March 25, 1937. "I have engaged a student to look up all the archaeology; this will leave me more time to perfect the text, without running the risk of misspellings and faulty renderings of the archaeological matter." On March 30 Mann answered her detailed queries seriatim:

First of all, I must answer your questions:

1) and 2) The *Berge Baumgarten* are the Carmel Mountains, which are called *Kirmil* in Hebrew.

3) *Das Sinnig-Heilige* should be translated as simply and literally as possible. *Sinnig* is a word that includes the meaning of notable, meaningful, and allusive. It will probably not have a complete equivalent in English. It would be most important to have the English word carry the idea of allusion, reference, and to continue with the word "holy."

Pages 28, 29. *Lobgold* is the German for an Egyptian word signifying the golden gifts and distinctions which Pharaoh, as he stood at the so-called "presentation window," threw down to his deserving courtiers and dignitaries while the people acclaimed him. These were not distinctions, orders of merit as we understand them, even though certain military distinctions had this character. The gifts included gold chains and other articles of jewelry which were worn as signs of reward and were called *Lobgold*.

Page 47. *Gottesleid* is one of the numerous word combinations used in the novel, as for example *Gottesverlegenheit*. Its meaning is a sorrow imposed by the deity and suffered for God, and at the same time a grief about God, for God's sake.

Page 17. *sodass* and *auf dass* designate the contrast between "resulting from" and "for the purpose of."

Page 49. *Wider den Stachel löken* is an archaic Lutheran form for the word *lecken* and is used particularly in this situation. This is derived from the simile of an oxen driven on by a prong lying on the plow. As he strikes out against the point of the prong, he feels it even more sorely. The other meaning of *lecken* or *löken* is to jump, to dance, to strike out. I hope there is a corresponding expression in English. The meaning of the phrase is to strike out in spite of the self-inflicted pain.

Page 72. *Hausbetreter.* This designation for the priests is not of my making. It comes to me from Orientalist lierature. The priests were actually named thus, meaning that they were the ones who had access to the house of God, not only to the antechamber but into the innermost shrine.

Page 97. *plieräugig, plierig,* a somewhat vulgar German word for red, inflamed eyes filled with mucus.

Page 67. *Krieger der Höhe.* This is an allusion to Joseph's dream in the second volume, his heavenly journey with the eagle on which he encounters armor-clad angels, who are called Warriors of the High Places. He sees the Egyptian soldiers at the gates and the portcullis as a realization, as it were, of his dream journey above the earth.

Page 71. *Kniekehle.* This applies to the Egyptian apron which is here not merely an apron covering the front but a garment covering the hips, a kilt. This is cut according to the prevailing fashion, in this case shorter in front than in the back, where it hangs down to the hollow of the knees.

Page 93. *Reine Kanten.* The word *rein* here has the meaning of sharp, clean, clear. Goethe uses the same word with the same meaning, as for example *rein genau,* clear and exact.

On July 6, 1937, he answered another series of questions from his translator:

I must not postpone answering your last questions any longer. They have been lying here too long already.

Page 56. *Halljahre.* It will scarcely be possible to find an

English equivalent. This signifies a time unit, seven times seven years at the end of which there is (in theory) a year of leisure, a sabbatical year. Your best solution would be to use the concept of an anniversary, a year of celebration, having somewhat the sense of the German *Jubeljahr*.[5]

Page 161. *Austritte Auferstehungen,* these are the pyramids, whose Egyptian appellation signifies a seceding from the earth, together with the idea of resurrection.

Page 181. *Ehrendudu,* a humorous usage in German connecting the proper name with the concept of dignity, honor. Where it refers to *Dudu* it has, of course, ironic meaning.

Page 182. *Ehrenpusslicht.* I explained this word in a previous letter. It means a kind of decency, probity, with a trace of prudishness, pedantry. The ending is an old-fashioned German one; in modern usage it would read *ehrenpusslig;* the *t* is used by older German writers, who often end with *cht*.

Page 206. *Dem reinen Erforderniss gefügig.* Fate yields to the simple intellectual demand and fulfills it.

Page 361. *schnatzen*—an archaic word meaning to comb, found particularly in Grimm's fairy tales.

Page 344. *Körigkeit*—the rut of the donkey.

Page 420. *ausgepicht*—crafty, cunning.

Page 431. *Amun's Empfängerin*—in a sexual sense. The queen receives the god, by whom she is made pregnant.

Page 534. *Im verspielten Zugleich,* explained in the previous letter.

Page 705. *Sagte sie ordinär.* Tabubu says in a vulgar tone, "That's enough," a common expression which departs from the elevated tone of the rest.

After she had translated *Doctor Faustus,* Mrs. Lowe was asked by an interviewer, Harvey Breit of *The New York Times Book Review,* whether she used a German-English

[5] In English we have the simple "jubilee."

dictionary. "I use a whole reference shelf," she replied. "Sometimes I refer directly to Dr. Mann. The question makes me laugh. 'Look up words?' See here, I've been translating since I was a girl. The words themselves are simple. . . . Translating Dr. Mann is a great privilege, also a greater chore than anybody realizes, except maybe Dr. Mann himself. The key to one of his sentences may lie in an adjective. To make English out of it you have to shift it to a noun, or maybe you can't shift it at all. Translation isn't just translation. It's work. I spent about a year on *Doctor Faustus* and weeks of collateral reading on the subject of music alone. The result isn't perfect, I know. The critics won't fail to point that out."

In this interview she pointed out a key difficulty in working with another language: "It sometimes also happens that a foreigner, however fluent his English, will not know *all* the implications of an English word and thus consider its use in an English sentence as incorrect. I once had a discussion on this point with a very great, very modest genius [probably Einstein], who could not believe that the German word *Erkenntniss,* translated, had in English, as in German, many shades of meaning. The same is true with English renderings of German words, my own included."

"We fully understand the immense difficulties of the task you have undertaken and, without any knowledge of the details, know how to value the work that you are doing," Katia Mann wrote to Helen Lowe on May 21, 1937. "Because T.M. knows full well what these demands are, he had the idea of entrusting a smaller book to someone else. But if you feel that you can translate *Lotte in Weimar* [*The Beloved Returns*] without great delay on the *Joseph,* it would be preferable and most desirable for him to have you do it."

Exhausting though the translating was, Mrs. Lowe took great pleasure in it, particularly in the Prelude to Jacob, "a rarely beautiful prose poem," she wrote. "So is the chapter 'Joseph Stands before Potiphar' in *Joseph in Egypt*. I am exceedingly enthusiastic about these two chapters; I cannot rejoice in them enough."

Despite her ten-year stint of eight hours of work each day on *Joseph*, Mrs. Lowe has little to say about it in "On Translating Thomas Mann." Nor, inexplicably, did she append a Translator's Note to this massive epic, which reached the length of 2,100 pages in German, 1,207 in English. She did comment privately on *Joseph in Egypt* in terms which give a key to understanding how she approached each massive book of the series: "I feel this time that there is some lack of spontaneity, more labour—but of course I may change my mind about this," she wrote to Alfred Knopf on March 11, 1936, after reading 600 pages, "since he does get his effects by sheer weight, and I can never tell whether he has really got them until I have been over the whole intensively." She certainly did change her mind, for on May 23, 1937, she wrote to Mr. Knopf: "I consider this volume one of the very greatest feats of the imagination which I know in literature. It is heavy-going in spots, and redundant, and will certainly be marred, in the English version, by the difficulties I speak of. But it is really gorgeous in its scope and power."

Mann continued to encourage her in this formidable task of translation. After the second book had been published in German and English, he wrote on May 24, 1935: "The excellent reception accorded *Young Joseph* by the press has pleased me immensely, and I do not fail to attribute a large share of this success to your skillful translation." And when, in 1948, the four books were published in a single volume he noted in the Foreword: "Here, then, is the whole work in a single binding, in Helen Lowe-Porter's admirable translation—an achievement of loyalty and devotion which this woman would not have been able to accomplish without faith in the worthiness of her task."

These words were written by Mann, when, after ten years in the United States, he had a good working command of English. His eldest daughter, Erika, quite bilingual, noted that "whenever possible [Mrs. Lowe] followed the intentions of the author. When asked by the press whether she had any specific problems, she answered: 'The Germans are too anxious to impress their German style on English. I want to get rid of the German because English is what I want it to be.' And yet her translation corresponds with the German original sometimes to an amazing degree" (*Briefe:* 1937–47, p. 701).

Mrs. Lowe so threw herself into her work that she made a promise to herself never to send a translation to the publisher unless she felt as though she had written the book herself. To do this she had to share with the author an attitude toward thought as it affects one's own way of life—*Lebensauffassung,* in a word. Certainly from the start Mann and Mrs. Lowe shared a similar cultural and literary point of view. In "On Translating Thomas Mann" she wrote:

Joseph in Egypt fascinated me. I find it T.M.'s greatest imaginative feat to that date and think its power and scope have never had justice from the reading public. He so early

28

became a "high-brow" author! The good work of his publishers and publicity agents so early made it imperative that everybody must buy him who wanted to be thought intellectual that he sold very well, though not overwhelmingly. Probably only a small proportion read, of those who bought. Alfred Knopf once said to me, "You see, Tommy does not know that everything is a racket." This cynicism did not prevent Alfred from feeling that T.M. was really great—nor did it me; so we were both exceedingly glad to make our respective contributions to the fame which otherwise he might have had to wait for in America, and in fact has never had in England, though he has there by now a discriminating if not a very large public.

Sometimes, she noted, "I did not feel quite at home in the more cloudy abstractions, also in some of the many long and very 'German' essays on Richard Wagner. This of course was due to my own lacks." But she had an even greater problem than the abstractions to face—the best way to reach a language which would be acceptable on both sides of the Atlantic. Kenneth Burke's translation of "Death in Venice" had been rejected in London as "too American." Mrs. Lowe had lived in Germany and Italy for years before World War I, and in Oxford and London for some twenty years; yet she was American born and educated—a splendid combination to lend an international tone to English style. The reception of her translations was superb in America—somewhat less so in England.

"The English reviews [of the first two volumes of the *Joseph*] were perfunctory," she noted in "On Translating Thomas Mann."

My name was occasionally mentioned, with a word or so, "damning with faint praise." What interested and pleased me was that my vocabulary was not spotted as American, this being a point always brought out by English reviewers if they get half a chance. I have throughout been forced—since the English version was for both markets—to emasculate the style, in some degree, taking care to write only what would be acceptable literary usage on both sides of the ocean. I came in time to follow the rule that no word or idiom should be used which was not intelligible, even if unfamiliar, to both publics. . . . I could and did use both definitely English and definitely American words and idioms; but they had to be understandable to both sides and good literature as well. And they must have local flavor, either English or American. Sometimes the English or American editor or critic would query or alter a word or phrase on the ground that it was not understandable. When that happened in conversation I always accepted the negative but almost never the positive criticism. It seems few people realize that a character in a novel *must speak in character;* they almost never suggested the right word, while spotting the wrong one.

Mrs. Lowe was to find another advocate of her ability in translating *Joseph* in Dorothy Canfield Fisher, then one of the judges of the Book-of-the-Month Club. On March 13, 1934, Mrs. Fisher wrote Mr. Knopf:

I think the translation of the Mann book is excellent. I read it with admiration for the skill and endurance of the translator, who must be very weary of the task. But I wonder—just on the general subject of translations, whether it isn't legitimate to make some of these slight changes in the style of the original which would bring it more within the spirit of the language into which it is set? For example, when the German sentences are notably longer and more involved than any now constructed by people writing in English, would it be a crime to break them up into shorter ones?

This translation does succeed remarkably in preserving the quality of the German original without sacrificing English clarity.

Mrs. Lowe was pleased with this tribute and replied to Mr. Knopf on March 30, 1934:

Many thanks for sending me Mrs. Fisher's comments on *Joseph*. Yes, of course—there are these two schools of translation: the one which believes that the right method is to reproduce the atmosphere of the foreign style by preserving very exactly the wave length, so to speak, the etymological significance of words, etc.; and the one which feels that it is insulting to an author who is worth translating to render his style into a sort of bastard English. I belong with Mrs. Fisher to the second school. I also think that—theoretically—every work of style, in a foreign language, can be (save for dialect, which presents certain special problems) rendered into a work of style in another tongue. But to do this the principle of substitution must be freely employed: i.e., getting the special effect of the original in one place if the resources of the language fail to produce it in another. In short, all translation is a kind of sleight-of-mind trick. You must draw off the reader's attention from weak points by concentrating on other ones. It is a psychological problem. Has Mrs. Fisher seen the version of the "Dinah" chapter of *Joseph* made by Ludwig Lewisohn? It appeared in the Paris magazine *This Quarter*. Also there is the work of Scott Moncrieff, a fine scholar. But both these men use the first method, I feel. As a matter of fact, in translating much of Dr. Mann, I have felt it sensible to break up the sentences or even to transpose them—the beginning of "Death in Venice" is a good example. But in *Joseph* I have not found it necessary, on the whole. I hope Mrs. Fisher did not want to deprive us of the glorious roll of that sentence in the Prelude to *Joseph*, beginning "Young Joseph, for instance," and going on for a whole page! I did try to reproduce its sonority in the English, but perhaps I failed.

While the writing and translating of the *Joseph* was proceeding, Mann would turn out essays—even the longish novel *Lotte in Weimar*—and Mrs. Lowe would turn them into English. It was in the process of doing the essays on political matters, such as "An Appeal to Reason" (1930), "Europe Beware" (1935), "I Stand with the Spanish People" (1936), "An Exchange of Letters" (1936), and "Culture and Politics" (1939), that Mann and Mrs. Lowe grew closer on a political *Weltanschauung*. She felt more and more strongly that she really understand and sympathized with Mann's life philosophy, or *Lebensauffassung*, that she was a part of it, in fact. At one point in the Thomas Mann-Helen Lowe relationship, Dr. Lowe snorted: "Helen, you're really married to Mann, considering what you've given to him." Perhaps Dr. Lowe felt that his wife was unduly influenced by Mann, for he found her writing "too intellectualized and ethereal." Her poetry he liked but her prose seemed to him to be "cold and detached." Thomas Mann himself, after twenty years of personal and literary association with her, wrote to Erich von Kahler: "I consider Mrs. Lowe not as a reader; she is a silent instrument who never utters a sound" (*"Die Lowe betrachte ich nicht als Leserin; sie ist ein schweigendes Instrument, tut nie einen Mucks"*) (*Briefe: 1937–47*, p. 431).

Such perfect understanding and accord had not always prevailed. From early youth, Mrs. Lowe had been on the liberal, even the radical, side of social and political matters. In Towanda, her birthplace, although she came from a long line of English settlers and should have taken her place on the side of the Republican ruling class, she was influenced by an earnest reformer and during a strike was appalled by the brutality of the management-police war against the strikers, so that she sided with the workers, and from then on fought against any assertion of privilege. An Anglo-Saxon Protestant, she had married a Jew over the protests of her family. After years of living in Europe, she became truly international in thought, word, and deed; only her accent betrayed her as a small-town American. Outwardly unemotional, inwardly she was torn by emotional loves and hates—love of the common man, hatred of the upper-class exploiter, of tyranny and privilege in any form. The Sacco-Vanzetti case, which dragged on from 1920 to 1927, moved her so deeply that she became physically ill when Sacco and Vanzetti were executed. The Russian Revolution seemed to her like the dawn of a new workers' paradise. In 1936 she made her pilgrimage to the Soviet Union to watch the system in action. Perhaps the contrast between theory and practice inoculated her against Communism, for she never joined the Party. For Fascism and Nazism she had nothing but contempt.

Thomas Mann, on the other hand, was in his youth a decidedly conservative German bourgeois, unlike his brother Heinrich, who believed firmly in the superiority of Western European democracy. During World War I, when Heinrich was in exile, the brothers had a spirited correspondence about their political differences, culminating in Thomas's *Reflections of a Non-Political Man*, which he described in *A Sketch of My Life* as "a quixotic and discursive defense of bourgeois romanticism, of nationalism, of the German side of the War." His bourgeois background and his artistic principles, he admitted, had "made a reactionary of me, or at least made me appear in that light for the moment. For at heart the book was far more of a developmental novel, far more of an experiment than a political manifesto. . . . Scarcely was the book finished in 1918 when I disassociated myself from it, a separation made easy for me in many ways . . ." When Mrs. Lowe offered to translate this work, Mann was alarmed, stating that much in it was of no import for the world of 1932. "There are large portions of this voluminous work that even to me now seem antiquated and out of date," he wrote to her on June 7, 1932. "And yet the book has elements that have remained valuable in my view and to which I adhere now as I did heretofore." His tastes and cultural traditions, he insisted, were "moral and metaphysical, not political and social." He had indeed come a long way since the *Kaiserzeit*.

"I have always begged T.M. to have the *Betrachtungen* translated, and he has always turned a deaf ear," Mrs. Lowe wrote to Alfred Knopf in July 1947. "I feel strongly that an artist's development is and must be organic. From that point of view, T.M. has come a long way since he started, but I think he should be proud of that instead of ashamed. Of course, he will never be 'political-minded.'"

In 1930 Mann addressed the "Appeal to Reason" to an audience some elements of which were in noisy opposition, as he explained in the Foreword to *Order of the Day*. ". . . its essential purpose was to make the German citizen understand that if German freedom and world peace were anyhow to be saved, his political station in the struggle was by the side of the working man. A bourgeois-socialist alliance, a compromise between democracy and socialism . . . might at that moment have saved Germany and the world from catastrophe."

In 1933 Hitler came to power and the Third Reich celebrated its inauguration with the burning of the Reichstag and with the *Juden-Boykott*. Mann was a marked man for his "Appeal to Reason," his other political addresses, his defense of Freud—"the Jewish pornographer," as Hitler called him—and for the subject of the Joseph series. That he should have chosen a Jewish subject during Hitler's rise to power added to the Nazi fury. And Frau Mann was half Jewish! Mann survived the first open attacks, wandering uneasily in Switzerland and France, but in 1936 his German citizenship was revoked, his Bonn doctorate was taken away, and his books were condemned to the flames in Berlin. Burned also were the books of his brother Heinrich and the works of Feuchtwanger, Bruno Frank, Wassermann, Arnold and Stefan Zweig, Remarque, Walter Rathenau, Einstein, and Hugo Preuss, the scholar who had drafted the Weimar Constitution. The ashes of these German books mingled with those of works by Jack London, Upton Sinclair, Helen Keller, Margaret Sanger, H. G. Wells, Havelock Ellis, Schnitzler, Freud, Gide, Zola, and Proust. That *Buddenbrooks* and *The Magic Mountain* should be burned as books "which act subversively on our future or strike at the root of German thought," as a Student Proclamation put it, was patently absurd. But Mann's life was a series of sometimes tragic ironies. His essay "Sufferings and Greatness of Richard Wagner" (Hitler's favorite composer) was violently abused in an appeal signed by, among others, Richard Strauss. German indignation at Mann grew so strong, indeed, that he was expelled from the Rotary International of Munich.

35

Fortunately, the Manns were in Lugano at the time of the first thunderbolt. "Thomas Mann is very depressed," Bruno Frank wrote Helen Lowe on April 20, 1933; "it is most fortunate that he has such splendid support in the person of the brave and intelligent Katia." Mann was quite reserved in his manner of reporting the catastrophe to Mrs. Lowe: in Arosa "we were overtaken by the news of the dreadful happenings in Germany," he wrote on April 1, 1933. "It is uncertain when and if I ever can return to Munich again. Perhaps a long exile is to be my fate. But do not speak of this, I beg you; I do not wish that there be any public talk of any intention of mine to leave Germany."

Directly she heard the news of the Nazi atrocities, Mrs. Lowe wrote Mann a letter, unfortunately lost, which gave him great comfort. On April 28, 1933, he replied:

My heartiest thanks for your splendid letter, which I received this morning. In recent weeks I have seen much brutality and ugly actions, but also much kind thoughtfulness and enduring gratitude, and on the whole I should not complain. Your letter is among the most comforting and heartening manifestations of kindly recognition of my life and work which I have ever received. When you are writing the preface to the new volume, all I ask of you is to retain in it the spirit and attitude of this letter. No more fitting introduction could be made to *Past Masters* than to characterize me as a writer with politico-cultural interests, as you did in your letter. You need not impose any restrictions upon yourself about my personal life. . . . I cannot imagine how I could be more compromised by your preface, even though you call a spade a spade.

In the longest foreword she ever appended to a Mann translation, Mrs. Lowe accepted his suggestion. Using the dialectic characteristics of his thought, she labeled Mann "a German author who is not less eminently 'Schriftsteller' [writer] than 'Dichter' [poet], to employ the antithesis habitual to his own thought." Mann, she knew, was working hard on the Joseph series, but this collection of miscellaneous essays led her to apply to him his own comment upon Wagner:

. . . what he is working on is never merely the task in hand, for everything else is weighing upon him and burdening the productive moment. The truth is that the organic nature of creation is a destiny—sometimes a nemesis—to the creator; and the quotation is applicable not merely to the technique of composition. For that technique must have inward harmony with what is in fact the source of Thomas Mann's special creative impulse and vitality: I mean his extraordinary power of coordinating his vision into all four points of time's compass—past and future, present and eternity. In this volume we shall escape few or none of the resultant antinomies of his habitual thought; yet be stimulated—as when we read the imaginative works—by the sense that we are rising far enough above them to get glimpses, as though from a great height, of their returning arcs.

. . . the present volume makes it clear that in him the cultural and political elements lie mingled, and that he accepts not only the fact but its national implications as well. . . . Indeed, hardly any of these essays escapes being in some sense an epitome of the spiritual and intellectual evolution of the author's nation. Though how far his own transcends theirs is illuminated by the following passage from the same essay: "Whereas originally the intellectual, in the shape of individualistic idealism, was bound up with the conception of culture, while the social concept, the class idea, never sensed its purely economic origins, it is in these days the latter that entertains toward the things of the mind far friendlier feelings than do its folk and middle-class opponents, whose conservatism has almost lost touch with the living spirit and its patent claims. I have . . . referred to the morbid and dangerous state of tension which has been set up in the world between mind, the height which the peak of humanity has already reached and made its own, and actual reality, and the state of enlightenment thought to be possible and attainable therein. It is the workers who display an undoubtedly stronger and more vital will toward the relaxing of this humiliating and dangerous tension than do their cultural opponents."

To what extent, however, we should guard against a too narrowly political interpretation of this paragraph can be seen from the close of the essay, where the whimsical yet serious suggestion is made that "Karl Marx read Friedrich Hölderlin." Here the poet in Dr. Mann triumphs over the "writer" and speaks again in the accents of the artist, whose mission it is to reconcile form and matter.

Mann wrote Mrs. Lowe on June 18, 1933, from his retreat in Sanary-sur-Mer, "La Tranquille":

You must have a very poor idea of my manners and my gratitude since I have failed until today to acknowledge the receipt of your letter with the enclosure of the preface,[6] nor have written you any comment on it. You must forgive me— between the day I received them and today we have moved once more and besides that, there has been—as you may well imagine—much preoccupation due to the present extraordinary circumstances.

I have read your preface, been much moved by it and am very grateful, and I am really greatly obliged to you for assuming this task as well as so many others and for

[6] To *Past Masters.*

accomplishing it with so much intelligence and grace. Everything you say is to the point—only one small matter seemed to me a bit doubtful. Where you speak of Lessing and the distaste of the German public for controversy, it almost seems as if I too wanted to eschew Lessing's polemics and wished to place myself on the side of the German point of view which I spoke of. That is somewhat misleading, since I mention this distaste and condemnation on the part of the Germans merely as an objective fact. In truth, I consider it rather a weakness of the German mentality and my sympathies are all on the side of the Lessing-type of writer, who not only experiences and recounts but judges and fights. I believe there should be no misunderstanding of this, all the more as only a few more lines will be required to remove any possibility of misinterpretation. . . .

We are happy to have resumed a private form of existence after the itinerant hotel-life of four months' duration. A few days ago we moved into this beautifully situated and comfortably equipped small house which we rented for the summer. Here we are at ease.

Dear Mrs. Lowe, please accept all my sincere thanks for your interest in and solicitude for my writings and my life. With heartiest greetings for you and your husband from my wife as from myself, I am . . .

Thus in 1933, the most shattering year of his hitherto placid life, Mann was comforted and strengthened by one whose cultural and political philosophy of life matched his own. For her part, Mrs. Lowe welcomed the political awakening of a man whose cultural and intellectual patterns she had so vastly admired. Truly their *Lebensauffassungen* matched and merged into one of the closest relationships between author and translator in any language.

After his exile from Germany, the burning of his books, and the seizure of his home and papers in Munich, Mann felt it necessary to speak out more forcefully even than in his "Appeal to Reason." As he points out in the Foreword to *Order of the Day* (1942), a collection of his essays and speeches on political and moral matters (all save two translated by Mrs. Lowe), his "political heart-searchings" were not "merely nine years old; they go back a generation, and it took not exile but the year 1914 and the moral and political world-crisis . . . to make of me an avowed and confessed combatant." The essay "Of the German Republic," he submitted, was "addressed particularly to the youth of Germany, in an effort to reconcile them with the domestic political results of the war of 1914–18; the voice of traditional culture sought to speak out on the side and in favor of the new necessities; to give democracy a gloss of the familiar by linking it with German romanticism." "Europe Beware," written after the democracies had supinely let Japan march into Manchuria and Italy into Ethiopia, found few hearers in 1935, when "Peace in Our Time" was the watchword. In 1936, the first year of the Spanish Civil War, he wrote "I Stand with the Spanish People." In 1937 he predicted "The Coming Victory of Democracy"; in 1938, the year of the appeasement of Hitler at Munich, he thundered in "This Peace" against the weak-kneed diplomats who had sold out Czechoslovakia. In that year he left Europe for the United States and applied for American citizenship.

Outstanding, perhaps, among these political documents is "An Exchange of Letters" [7] (*Ein Briefwechsel*, 1936),

[7] The letter from the Dean of the University of Bonn, announcing the revocation of Mann's doctorate and his reply.

which rang out like a tocsin to rouse both Germans and citizens of the democracies. Its concluding line gives the tone of anger and compassion in which it was written: "God help our darkened and desecrated country and teach it to make its peace with the world and with itself!" Mrs. Lowe agreed that "it was a noble document and displayed full knowledge and lofty indignation over conditions in Germany," as she wrote in "On Translating Thomas Manns"; "less, however, of those in England and France, for it referred to the attitude in the government of those countries, as 'that of the physician toward a fever patient' . . . The words struck a chill to my heart, and I wrote to T.M. begging him to come to England and meet some of the writers . . . In reply I had a kindly but complacent letter beginning, '*Ihr sehr pessimistisch gefärbter Brief*'" ("Your rather pessimistic statements").

Actually she had written on February 14, 1937:

I am moved, though with great humility, to write to you about this pamphlet. I found it eloquent, stirring and very fine, and as a statement of conditions in Germany most valuable propaganda. But as I turned it into English and pondered it I felt sad. I wondered if you do not move in too rarefied an air, among thoughts of too lofty an enlightenment, for the necessary ingredient of cynicism to find enough place in your political outlook. I felt the same when I heard Jules Romains speak here last winter. I know the point of view: I have encountered it here in England, where there are so many of the best of those whom Germany has exiled and misused. England seems so safe, so high-minded, so well-founded in the maturity of her political tradition; it is so natural a thing that those whom she has welcomed should idealize her. I do beg you not to do this. The rulers of England are not what you call them: physicians who are trying by tact and forbearance to bring a morbid patient back to health and reason. Their job is to preserve the Empire and the system on which it rests. They are not *au dessus de la mêlée*. They would far rather preserve Hitler and see Franco win, than take any step against either which might tend to encourage other forces dangerous to their existence either within Britain or without. At bottom, and in the last resort, their sympathies must lie with Hitler, Mussolini and Franco. I seem to state this categorically; actually, it is the conclusion of a process of reasoning followed by large bodies of people both in this country and elsewhere. Such people . . . were disturbed by events in Manchuria, Abyssinia and now in Spain. Even people previously unaffected by radical ideas, were moved to study the political and economic backgrounds of those events, and they could not help seeing that the English government has refrained from action because it feared to upset the economic system which has built up its predominance. They were driven to link up their conclusions, and the pretty disgraceful history of bargaining among the powers, with the whole Left theory of economics—and so took a big step towards hostility against the imperialist powers, including the government of their own country. Their political ideology changed . . . and they saw, which is of course a commonplace to you, that the struggle is not between nations but between forces within each nation. They adopted, or were confirmed in, the international-socialistic point of view. I am rather surprised at my own presumption in begging you to do the same: in the words of St. Paul, to "come over into Macedonia and help us."

This letter, which he found "most interesting," Mann answered on March 9:

That not everything in England is as it should be has been my own experience *en miniature*, as it were, in the matter of the

"Exchange of Letters" with Germany; everywhere else, except in England, this has appeared twice, as a news item in the papers, and as a monograph in its entirety. There must be some profound reason for that, the reason being simply that matters like this should not be noticed, should preferably be ignored. Your rather pessimistic statements confirm this belief, though, nevertheless, the important fact of English rearmament remains, a measure surely directed against Italian adventure and boasting, and even more clearly pointed at the threats coming from the Germany of today. The fact of this rearmament is the most important event occurring within recent years; it implies a kind of awakening which is of course welcomed by France with all signs of great relief. In my letter I have tried to show that war is out of the question for this German state for internal reasons; but that it is English rearmament which makes war impossible for external reasons. Your government [8] therefore is quite correct in claiming that the tremendous sacrifices it demands from the people do serve the cause of peace. It is certain that such an increase of power on the part of the state must have its inner-political repercussion, but I believe that the paramount factor is to check the despicable regime in Berlin which is challenging the world. It is clear that its only reason for being would be war, and if war is made impossible it must perforce sooner or later collapse.

After this serious political letter, the balance of their correspondence in 1937 was on fine points of translation of German words in the third volume of the Joseph series.

When, in 1938, Mann came to America, as Mrs. Lowe records in "On Translating Thomas Mann,"

[8] Mann apparently thought her to be English. She remained an American citizen.

he greeted me, as he put out his hand, by saying, *"Doch, Sie hatten Recht"* ["Well, you were right"]. Which was handsome of him. It is not surprising that T.M. had no great knowledge of English politics; rather more so that he did not estimate the French scene with greater perspicuousness. . . . On both accounts, however, the weakness has to be laid to Mann's earlier indifference to politics in general. A characteristic of the *Kaiserzeit*, as we all know; and not the only time or place where men of intellect and ideals have found it beneath them to concern themselves with politics. The more the time has cried out for brave intellectuals, the more time has exposed the schism in their thinking.

Mrs. Lowe did distinguish between the Mann of the *Kaiserzeit* and the Mann of the "Appeal to Reason":

His familiar antinomies, *Kultur* and *Civilization*, are as he uses them political terms in the international sense. . . . I have no patience with those hecklers who sought to accuse him of fascist leanings. His, I feel, is the long, half-conscious evolution of a creative mind, in a period of such drastic *"Umwertung aller Werte"* [complete flip-flop] that it must on the contrary be set down to T.M.'s credit that he has not been deterred from marking his stages and making his profession of them as he reaches them.

In 1939, in an interview with *Life* magazine, Mann made his final profession of his conversion to the total involvement of the artist with the world:

I must regretfully own that in my younger years I shared that dangerous German habit of thought which regards life and intellect, art and politics as totally separate worlds. In those days we were all of us inclined to view political and social matters as non-essentials that might as well be trusted to politicians. And we were foolish enough to rely on the ability of these specialists to protect our highest interests.

In 1935, Klaus, Mann's oldest son, who was to become an American soldier in the crusade against Hitler, published an open letter to the American people, asking them to consider the plight of the German refugees. Mrs. Lowe wrote a sensitive and sensible "Open Letter to Klaus Mann," which apparently never found publication.

You appeal to our imaginations. You ask us to realize, more intensively and more actively, the sufferings and the predicament of those who are exiled, voluntarily or involuntarily, from a Germany where, even if they remained, they could no longer be at home. It is, you would say, the Fatherland which has forsaken you, not you the Fatherland.

It is the Fatherland—all that you mean by the word—which temporarily or permanently has evacuated the soil that gave it birth. It is not there any more. What there exists of it, you would even say, you bear about with you in your hearts, each of you a piece of it, wherever you go.

It is this state of things that you ask us to realize, more intensively and more actively, by the power of our imaginations. Rightly you say that our human imagination is feeble. Some of us have not very much, in any active sense. But even without that, most of us have felt very sorry for you and have helped as generously as we could, out of ordinary kindliness (I will not discuss how much imagination goes to make up ordinary kindliness, or we shall be lost among definitions). As much help as possible has been given to lighten the material suffering of the exile—the kind of suffering that makes a kindly, well-fed man uncomfortable to think of. But that is not what you are talking about. It is something else you want of us. What is it we can do?

One thing we cannot do. We cannot, by any taking-thought

of ours, give you back your soil, your forests, your local idiom and childhood memories and traditions, your roots, your secure feeling that you were part of something and it was part of you. Your loss is irremediable.

But perhaps those gifted with imagination may be doing something else—and it may be the gist of what you mean. It is not pity—however active—that we feel for you, we who live in the other countries, whither you travel and "think to find that peace, unity and justice prevail." We are not sorry for you, any more than for ourselves, *really*. We suffer *with* you, instead; for ah, believe us, we are not any more "comfortable in our skins" than you are in yours. We have been uncomfortable for as long as you, and our discomfort is as little ephemeral as yours—(though it cannot of course be so poignant or occupy our consciousness as exclusively)—because at bottom it is the same discomfort. We are still at home; and far be it from us to minimize the pain of those who are physically not so. But there is a good deal of the exile about us too. We are uneasy, strange, apprehensive, angry, just like you. We see the oncoming perils and lie awake nights and think that beauty and justice and the spirit may be about to perish. Just like you. Is that any good to you? And our feelings will lead to action too—under your conditions. They are active forces. I can think of two men, both of high rank in the world of the mind, both members of "a certain race" who never in their lives have known any disability due to the fact. And they suffer *more* anguish of mind just because they have personally as it were got off scot-free. There must be many like them.

Indignation and shame and the sense of oncoming peril are constructive forces. But our solidarity with you has another aspect probably more constructive still; though it cannot lighten the individual burden of any of us sufferers save the few endowed with creative imagination in an almost superhuman degree. Such people can hearten themselves with the hope that something will come of the suffering, something probably quite worthwhile even dying for: I mean cooperation in the development of some ideal more consoling and more serviceable even than that of a Fatherland.

Mrs. Lowe had an arch sense of humor, and her reactions to Hitler were not always so poignant, as this letter of January 18, 1941, to *The New Yorker* magazine indicates:

It might interest you—in re article on Hexing Hitler—that it occurred to my daughter (Bice) and me to do the same thing, in Germany back in 1935. We got a tiny Hitler, about two inches high, out of a toy set, with movable right arm for heiling. As he was too tough to stick pins in, we decided to burn him (also quite good black magic, see D. G. Rossetti's "Sister Helen"—"Why did you melt your waxen man?"). But he would not burn. Made of asbestos. Just like the Germans— they think of everything.

In 1938 the Manns had come to America for his lecture tour. In view of the events in Europe—in 1938 Austria and Czechoslovakia had fallen victims of Hitler—they decided to remain in the United States and to apply for citizenship. "The pressure of events leaves no room for any joy in life," Katia Mann wrote to Mrs. Lowe on March 28, 1938, "the situation grows more hopeless day by day." The Manns then settled in Princeton for three years.

When Princeton University asked for a series of lectures in English, Mann applied for Mrs. Lowe's assistance, not only in translation, but also in pronunciation. This assistance she gave him, correcting his Teutonic accent on word after word ("bosom," for example came out as "bosóóm"). She and Dr. Lowe went to hear his inaugural lecture on

Goethe's *Faust* (included in *Essays of Three Decades*), of which she wrote their eldest daughter, Prue:

> He had come here two nights to read it aloud to me and get the words pronounced right; but alas, his sing-song is so very German that I, knowing the thing by heart as I did, had difficulty in understanding, and many people, I am sure, did not. Next time I will read it aloud to him instead. Woe! Woe! (or Whoe! Whoe! as T. Mann would say). He mentioned an 18th c. German critic named Pustkuchen, and obviously relished the name so much that I suggested he translate it "popover," to let the audience share the joke. He did—but alas! he called it "popeover."

Facing the problem of adapting himself and his family to the language and customs of his adopted country, Mann continued to write calmly about Joseph and his antique, alien culture; but he strengthened his cultural ties with Germany by undertaking the story of his culture hero, Goethe, and his lost love in *Lotte in Weimar* (*The Beloved Returns*). For the first time, the author and his translator were working together. The friendship between the Manns and the Lowes, initiated in Oxford, was made firm in Princeton, where Mann found as fellow-exiles such friends of the Lowes as Albert Einstein and Erich von Kahler. There were sympathetic evenings at the Lowes', where, for example, Mrs. Lowe read to the Manns an account of a performance at Oxford of the *Urfaust*, "by a company of young German actors." Perhaps to test Mann's social and political sympathies, she referred the piece "to the class and economic structure of society," and objected that "Goethe seemed nowhere to admit that the dice were loaded in Faust's favor as against Gretchen's. He had not, here, a strong sense of human values." Mrs. Lowe was

48

exhibiting her feminist as well as her social sympathies: "It was with a certain shock that I myself realized how Marxian my thinking was at that time. Or was it my Puritan ethics? I mean that I referred the piece to the class and economic structure of society."

Frau Mann was shocked at the irreverent treatment of the great Goethe, but Thomas Mann nodded his head in partial acquiescence. This nod led Mrs. Lowe to compare Goethe and Shakespeare in their treatment of women. "Shakespeare found women more *human* than Goethe did. There is scarcely a female in the big gallery of Shakespeare's women who *could* have been deserted. They are all too much *Mensch*. . . . The only point I am making is that age for age, class for class, genius for genius, Goethe's ideals were not so loftily human after all." To a certain extent, Mann agreed with his translator, for he had written in "Goethe as Representative of the Bourgeois Age":

In Gretchen's tragic fate, in the guilt of Faust, not a paragraph, not a social attitude, not an institution is attacked; here a poet merely discourses with the Eternal upon man's tragic lot. And so this same poet, as member of the Weimar Council of State, could sign the death-warrant of a young girl guilty of child-murder. He signed his name under the names of the other unpitying ministers, though the Duke himself would have shown her mercy. *"Ich auch,"* he wrote. I am not the first to find the fact almost as shattering as the whole of Faust.

In her preface to the translation of *The Beloved Returns*, which Mann found "extraordinarily successful and correct" (August 11, 1940), Mrs. Lowe commented tartly that "nothing human was foreign to [Goethe]—save the field of politics. He had contempt for the people—'when the masses fight, they are respectable; but their opinions are not delectable!'—and boasted that he had never had the misfortune to be in the opposition" (p. vii). In "On Translating Thomas Mann" she said:

> I began translating *Lotte in Weimar* during that last "peace" summer of 1939—in a rented house with a beautiful rose garden. . . . In general this was not a painful period, rather a rich one with profound human significance. Just accepting as background the certainty of horrors to come made all experience more vivid and precious.

She faced special difficulties in Chapter VII, which she conveyed to Mann, then on a lecture tour through Europe. "I have just received your card in which you acknowledge receipt of the 7th chapter," he answered on August 2, 1939,

and express your readily comprehensible anxiety at this vexatious piece of prose. I should like to allay your fears and ask you not to take the matter so tragically. "Take it easy!" as the saying goes. It will not be half as bad as it seems to you at first glance, and much research, which now appears to you to be necessary, can surely be omitted. As soon as we are both in Princeton again we can get together for one or more times, and I shall explain the passages to you which you marked when you went over the manuscript.

For that matter, I was already aware while writing this chapter that a foreign language could not express all the various points of the train of thought nor all the allusions which it carries with it. I acknowledge willingly that much must be omitted in translating and I believe that such omissions had best be left to the judgment and the feelings of the respective translator. . . .

I felt the need of sending you a word of comfort at once, as well as to excuse myself. It is clear that you will have to take great pains, but you must not worry too much about it. . . .

In a letter to his Hungarian translator, Jenö Gömöri, dated November 15, 1951, Mann spelled out the difficulty of translation:

It is generally known that lyric poetry [*Lyrik*] cannot really be translated. That this is also the case with more refined prose is known only to a few—most likely only the sensitive translators themselves, many of whom have complained to me about it. Such prose [*Prosa*] is usually perverted, its rhythm is destroyed, the subtle shades of meaning are lost, its inner intention, its mental attitude and intellectual atmosphere diverted up to the point of complete misunderstanding. This reminds me of the time when my American translator and friend, Helen Lowe-Porter, said to me while she was at work on the translation of *Lotte in Weimar,* deploringly, "I am committing murder!"

"Murder" she may have committed, but Mann knew enough English to find it first-rate "murder." In August 1940, when a German invasion of Britain seemed imminent, Mann wrote from Los Angeles to Mrs. Lowe about "*Our* book, the dear Lotte":

I could not possibly read the German book now, but I have looked over your translation a number of times and my conviction grows ever stronger that you have accomplished what is humanly possible: you have given this really untranslatable book the best possible translation. I also find the introduction, short and factual as it is, extraordinarily successful and correct. It will serve its purpose admirably.

How will the book be received? Let us hope for the

best. . . . There are a number of signs that the book may even stir up some excitement in this country. . . .

One of the disadvantages here is the strange lassitude [he added on a different note] which befalls me as it does other newcomers. It makes work harder for me than usual. In spite of this, I have completed the Indian legend-story [*The Transposed Heads*] during the first weeks here and can promise you the typescript shortly. I am curious to learn how you will like this queer production and what you will think of its chances in this country. I suppose that, after a due interval after the Goethe novel, a small volume can be made of it. . . . After that, it took only a few days to pick up again the dropped threads of the *Joseph* and to begin the final volume.

Of course, we have much work connected with the victims of events who are crying to us for help from various European countries. Among those in danger are my brother Heinrich and our son Golo. Nor are our efforts limited to the immediate family. Our place has become a kind of refugee office, and there is no end to telegrams and to all kinds of steps to be taken, though success only rarely repays the effort.

He concluded: "These lines are, above all, intended as an expression of thanks for what you have again accomplished for one of my works. For I know full well, as the results strikingly show, what great measure of care and empathy, so highly deserving of gratitude, you have put into your work" (August 11, 1940).

Mrs. Lowe had taken more pains, if that was possible, over Mann's "beloved Lotte" than over *The Magic Mountain* or the *Joseph:* she devoted several pages to it in "On Translating Thomas Mann":

. . . *Lotte in Weimar* was very difficult, especially the parts which use a stream-of-consciousness technique to portray the character of Goethe. I think them highly successful, for the reason that (a) nobody was ever better self-documented than Goethe and (b) another great representative of literary Germany had the imaginative power to present him as he was and lived and table-talked. But nobody save a last-generation literary German or professors of German literature in other countries could possibly appreciate the achievement. I worked hard on the English version, and had some help from a refugee, a former editor of the *Frankfurter Zeitung.* I doubt if the book was much read, and the translation when it was noticed at all was reviled, not greatly to my surprise. After all, every translator knows that translating is a sort of trick, a device like the sleight-of-hand operator's to attract attention to something in order to distract it from something else. There is a sense in which all art fits such a definition—witness the double sense in which the word itself can be used. So also word-craft. When we speak of the little art of translating I am content to have the word used in this double sense. On the other hand I please myself, privately, by thinking of it as a "mystery" in the archaic and now very modern literary sense.

As for *Lotte in Weimar:* the original is a period piece, and as such presented the usual difficulties. I hit on the idea of assimilating the style to the Weimar chapters in Thackeray's *Vanity Fair.* Critics found the result preposterous, awkward, stuffy, and so on. I cannot defend literary translation against the charge that it is a perverse pleasure, and that the translator would be better employed as a philologist or a language teacher. Everybody who ever writes verse or tries to turn a poem into another language than the original, knows that the result, in the measure that it is good as literature, is not the same poem. Try to translate Rilke, for instance! This must be so. Take a translation from Goethe: those happy, facile little lines written by him to commemorate the birthday of his friend the Arch-Duke Karl August:

53

Mit allem Schall und Klang
Der Transoxanen
Erkühnt sich unser Sang
Auf Deine Bahnen.
Uns ist für gar nichts bang
In dir lebendig
Dein Leben dauere lang
Dein Reich beständig.

Skilled, singable little lines! Dr. Mann quoted them on the fly-leaf of *Lotte in Weimar*. It was decided with his approval that they be left in the original. This is always the better plan, especially in a book like *Lotte in Weimar*, which completely misfires unless one knows something of German culture. A short time after it was published, a letter appeared in the *Saturday Review of Literature*, from Miss Caroline Newton, with an English version of the stanzas by no less a poet than W. H. Auden. I answered the letter by sending the version already made by me and not used. Both versions accordingly saw the light in the *Saturday Review of Literature*, and I give them here with the caution that I am, of course, not absurd enough to compare myself with Auden as either poet or scholar. After all, the original itself is only a smooth and practised little "occasional verse" such as a poet laureate writes to celebrate an anniversary of his liege: here is Auden's version:

Though conch and tribal gong
Howl in the marches,
Bold be our rebel song,
Thy courts and arches
Stand. We dread no wrong
In thee made able.
O may thy reign be long
Thy kingdom stable.

and here is mine:

> *Through all the bounce and blare*
> *Of border races*
> *Our song makes bold to fare*
> *Upon thy traces.*
> *We fear not any wrong*
> *In thee residing—*
> *Oh, may thy life be long,*
> *Thy realm abiding.*

It is clear that Auden's version is the work of a poet. It is eight lines of such verse as he might have written had he been a personal friend of, say, F.D.R. But it is not, I feel, in spirit or technique like the simple warm little patriotic Goethe lines. It does not seem eighteenth-century to me. Auden, I think, cannot be a translator, however hard he tries. He kept the first rule of a translator, to make, not a translation, which is "God bless us, a thing of naught," but did not keep the second (which is to keep the words and the spirit). Or am I all wrong?

This is probably the best place to set down a few comments on technical problems. Of course they apply only to translations from German into English, the field in which I have my only extended experience. I will not attempt to discuss the well-known fact that the German language is both more inflected and more explicit than the English, though German style has been subject in the nineteenth century to a slow simplification, as we know. It is the case that in English not only is inflection at a minimum, but also the train of thought is likely merely to suggest where the German follows through, explaining and expounding. The result is that English is easier to read—unless, of course, you are reading aloud. The German constructs more relative and subordinate clauses, with longer sentences, a different order. So the sentences, in order not to

55

produce a clumsy English, must be broken up—with the result that nobody is quite satisfied. English readers of a translation from the German complain that the sentences still need shortening, while the German author wishes they had not been tampered with. Let me interpolate here that English, perhaps I should say American, style tends to shorter and yet shorter sentences and paragraphs. We are in a great hurry today. Are our modern inventions responsible for the loss of leisure in written English? To return: sometimes the actual order not only of the words but of the thoughts, the logical sequence differs in the two languages. I recall receiving a scolding from a German refugee scholar for transposing the order of two paragraphs, because it seemed to me the transition would thus be less uneasy for an English ear. I will merely mention here cases where one must rely on the context to get the just translation for a "portmanteau" word like the famous German *Geist*. English has no single word for *Geist;* but it has its own portmanteaux, of course, for instance the very word already mentioned—*Art,* of which a German critic, however good a linguist, may not always be aware.

There is, again, the matter of dialect. I think it can only be faintly suggested, never localized in a different country. This is a distinct loss, of course. One way of dealing with it is by transferring the bad grammar—if there is any. I remember having difficulty with the local (Lübeck) tongue in *Buddenbrooks* and feeling dissatisfied with the result. Idioms, as distinct from dialect, do sometimes, happily, have exact correspondences in the two languages. Where they have not, I have often taken the liberty of using *in another place* the same kind of idiom, pun, or verbal play used by the German author. This will have the effect of reproducing the style in general, though I must concede that . . . the result is a portrait, not a photograph.

Again, it may sometimes happen that the original sentence

uses a verb, noun, or adjective where the idea only exists—or can only be adequately rendered in English—in a different part of speech. An entirely different sentence-structure results —and another instance of what Bernard Shaw called "translators' little treacheries." These must be called the rigidities of the translators' job, whereas there are relaxations as well: I mean chances actually to translate etymologically—the idea, in other words. A striking illustration of what I mean is Dr. Mann's *The Holy Sinner*, the setting of the tale being the coast of Flanders, the time anywhere between the seventh and eleventh centuries, giving an unexampled and delightful opportunity for linguistic fidelity.

She wrote a long letter to their publisher, Alfred A. Knopf, on November 11, 1943:

I think perhaps it might be useful for me to write to you about the *Lotte* translation and my own point of view on the criticisms of it. The *"Kleinkunst"* of translation is, I think, like all art, a "mystery" in the guild sense; and all real translators have their own notions about how it ought to be practised. Did you know that Goethe once wrote a charming, though rather conventional poem about it, beginning: *"Einst pflückte ich einen Blumenstrauss"* [once I gathered a bouquet of flowers]? It was sent to me, years ago, by Bruno Frank, by way of graceful thanks for what he thought I had done for him. A good deal has been written, especially in England, about the translation from ancient tongues, the finest said by Matthew Arnold in *Essays in Criticism;* but little, so far as I know, about the translation of modern ones. A good lecture by Hilaire Belloc, and some passages I think in George Moore, are all I can recall just now.

When I receive one of Dr. Mann's works to translate, what I try to do is to read it, not merely to get the sense but the flavor, the mood and tempo, the atmosphere. Translators, like reviewers, are often pressed to do hack and hasty work. But no one likes to do this, and all translators know that the really happy and just rendering of a word or phrase does not always come at once, and ought to be waited for if necessary. I am speaking, of course, of translations of literary works. The reviewer is in a little happier case: he may use his own ideas, the poor translator has only the Word. Well, then, I try to decide whether the book has its peculiar characteristics of style and atmosphere which it would be my duty to try to represent. The *Lotte*, in my judgment—good or bad—was a period piece; and we had a wide range of beautiful English prose that might evoke for the reader the same atmosphere which the original does for the German one. I do not mean that I wanted to give the English version the style of any particular writer. I only read—or reread—a lot, to get it in my ear. I tried Coleridge for the metaphysical Riemer chapter. I confess that the opening sentence of *The Beloved Returns* is, in its word-order, reminiscent of the first sentence of *Vanity Fair:* "When the present century was in its teens, and on one pleasant sunshiny June morning"—I think that bears the hallmark of genius. I thought I would eliminate the recurrent German "which," clumsy to an English ear; I would seek to make the clauses glide smoothly into each other, as in matchless Jane Austen, who was one model for me, though not a Victorian. I would take a good deal of pains with the vocabulary, occasionally using a dated word, ending, phrase, or cadence. The German of the Napoleonic period employed French words and phrases. I would take advantage of the fact, not only where the author did, but also just occasionally where the French was apter than the English. And when I got this well into my ear and feeling, I would use it to clothe as meticulous, supple, and intuitive a rendering of the original as I possibly could. I think there might easily be a difference of opinion about the result. Perhaps it is precious; but at any rate it was deliberate. It is clear that the author of *Budden-brooks, Der Zauberberg,* the Joseph series, and *Lotte* would and did fuse his matter and his style into an organic whole. The translations ought to show an effort on the part of the translator to do the same. Anyone reading the little preface would see that my own style is different, not quite so "stuffy Victorian." *Lotte in Weimar* is indubitably a highly literary performance; it behooved the translator to try to get the same effect. That seems to me a right position to take up, in translating works of art. I cannot think a creative artist would be glad to see his delicate balance quite upset, his true marriage of thought and word turned into something which, however word-accurate, had ceased to be literature at all. That is throwing the baby out with the bath. And herein lies the Scylla of translators: the Charybdis would be the failure to give a faithful rendering of the sense. It is very hard to avoid them both. The translator steers as warily as may be; but however conscientious, he is likely to be blamed for steering on to one or the other. And speaking of blame: it has happened to me more than once that a reviewer of something I have done will ignore or slight the translation, and then write me a personal letter full of high praise.

This letter is already very long. I could write for pages about the problems of translators, the trade secrets which are of interest only to the guild. I have often thought that translation is a trick, and a good translator like a sleight-of-hand artist who must concentrate the reader's attention on something so that the latter will not notice something else which might spoil the effect. Such a "something else," for instance, is dialect. In *Buddenbrooks* there is a good deal of the Hamburghese used by longshoremen. Little could be done with it. To translate it into something comparable in England or this country was to introduce a local flavor that must inevitably make the reader think of the English or American scene, and that would jar.

Dealing with the German second person singular is under the same circumstances a tricky thing. A special difficulty for me has been that one translation has had to serve both the English and the American market. I had to try to achieve a sort of blurring of places and time which might well emasculate the style. Sometimes, however, one gets a lucky break: one could do—or try to do—whole chapters of the Joseph series in the prose of the King James version, or what one fondly imagined to be that. On the other hand, the seventh chapter of *Lotte* sets a practically impossible task, but for another reason altogether: it is a weave of literary allusions and quotations intelligible at best only to a middle-aged German of a certain culture and scarcely to any modern American save a German professor. I notice that some reviewers just omitted this chapter, though it is the key one of the book, and full of fascinations.

Another principle that I have, which I may just mention, because a lot of people mightn't agree with it, is what I call substitution. Each language has its own genius, though some are more alike than others in their genesis and growth. I may come on a fine idiomatic or allusive phrase in the German and find that the English just does not lend itself to the same effect. But perhaps another sentence elsewhere in the text can display the same kind of literary virtue in English, where it did not happen in the German. I consider it justifiable to take advantage of the fact. But it makes the job of the reviewer harder. He has to look at the whole, not pick out sentences, if he means to judge the translation at all. In the matter of length: it is a fact, according to Hilaire Belloc, and it seems to stand to reason, that a translation will tend to be longer than its original, because in the nature of things it will be less idiomatic. The principle of substitution is a help here, as well as enriching the style. I might speak of another translator's problem here: the whole question of the relation of the thought and the word in the artist's mind. But that would land us in the realm of metaphysics. In general, I always imagine to myself that a perfect transference from German to English is theoretically possible, even in poetry. When, as mostly, I do not achieve it, I just think I am at fault. I find it better, though sterner, to work in this spirit.

May I thank you here for the support and friendliness you have always shown me in my work for Dr. Mann?

In "On Translating Thomas Mann" she made this comment on the practical aspect of translation: "It is practically always a part-time job, an avocation. As a full-time occupation, I hardly think it could earn a living. The pay is poor and grows poorer by reason of the justified improvement in typists' fees, so that the translator must do his own typing or his money payment is small indeed." Mrs. Lowe's comments upon the sad financial lot of the translator should warn off any who believe that a full-time translator can earn a living wage. She states that she received $750 for the two large volumes of *Buddenbrooks*. In 1929 she was offered by Alfred Knopf, who remained Mann's publisher and hers to the end, £1 per 1,000 words for the first Joseph volume. This was cut to 15 shillings for "Mario and the Magician" in 1930, but went up to a guinea per 1,000 in 1932. *Young Joseph* came to 100,000 words and 100 guineas. In 1935 Mr. Knopf offered $3.00 per 1,000, but by 1942 the fee had risen to $5.25 per 1,000. In 1944, when the Book-of-the-Month Club took *Joseph the Provider*, Mr. Knopf upped the rate to $8.00 per 1,000, and she was getting $10 per 1,000 in 1951 for *The Holy Sinner*, her last Mann translation. Through the years Mrs. Lowe had sometimes to hire research assistants and typists. As her physical powers failed, she felt the necessity of hiring a full-time secretary-companion. This expense she asked Mr. Knopf to shoulder, but he explained that the cost of translation was taken out of royalties to the author, and that she would have to come to some arrangement with Mann, who was totally dependent upon his royalties. Mrs. Lowe rather sadly accepted the facts of publishing and wrote to Mr. Knopf: "I have never had the feeling that you were not treating me well and kindly" (April 8, 1945). Although there were moments of tension between Mrs. Lowe and Mann, starting with his temporary decision to have *The Magic Mountain* translated by a man, there was never any real tension between her and Alfred Knopf. Blanche Knopf also remained one of Helen Lowe's staunch supporters throughout their relationship.

We are fortunate to have an eyewitness account of Mrs. Lowe's manner of working as she translated *Lotte in Weimar*. Judith Heller lived with Mrs. Lowe from time to time, and as they were both bilingual, they were of the greatest assistance to one another. "Helen would of course read over most carefully the German version, noting all kinds of linguistic difficulties and involved syntactical stumbling blocks," writes Mrs. Heller.

Then she would usually read some clarifying book on a related subject, especially if the material was strange, as in *The Transposed Heads*. Then, steeped in the subject, she would complete a rough draft in manuscript, translating more or less literally from the German. This she would let lie for some time and then take it up, to "English it," as she called it, going over this with improvement of phrase, corrections of sense, once, or if necessary twice. At the start she would type the whole long business, from the second draft on, herself, and not until the Princeton days did she dictate to a secretary or have her corrected manuscript copied by a professional. The galleys would come back to her for correction and she would correct them while lying on her bed, supporting the paper on an old cracked board, with dictionaries lying to right and left. When she translated *Lotte in Weimar*, the German of which was in many places outmoded, we sat for three days in her little hotel room in New York. I held the German book while she read her English translation very slowly from her completed draft and asked for criticism of meaning and form. When she worked on the *Doctor Faustus*, with its strangely archaically constructed scene with the apparition of the devil, I put together for her a bibliography of archaic English biblical texts that she might consult on language oddities. It was this way with every piece of work she undertook, for she wished to enter into the very heart of the author's intention and to understand his sources, to make them her own, before she undertook to transpose his thoughts and words into her own language. In this sense she was a real creator, keeping step with Dr. Mann. It is this which makes her work unique, a true work of literary art.

As we have seen, Mann was thoroughly satisfied with the translation of *Lotte in Weimar*, but at least one American reviewer deemed the translation "stilted," whereupon Erwin Panofsky, a world-famous art historian and a German refugee professor at the Princeton Institute for Advanced Study, wrote to Alfred Knopf on October 4, 1940, in defense of Mrs. Lowe's version:

You will, I hope, forgive a German-born American, unknown to you even by name, for writing you a letter about your publications of the works of Thomas Mann in English.

What prompts me to do this is, in the first place, a curious coincidence. Being fairly well acquainted with Mann's works in German I had given myself the somewhat perverted pleasure of reading them in English, when I came across Mr. Lewis Gannett's review of *The Beloved Returns* in the *Herald Tribune,* which I do not read as a regular habit. In the second place, I have been trying for a number of years to write my own books and articles in English and can thus claim some experience with the problem of "translating," that is, of transferring a complex organism of thought from one language into another. I say a "complex organism of thought" advisedly, for we must admit, I think, that an adequate translation of single words, even apparently simple ones, is *ipso facto* impossible. They can be rendered "wrong" if the translator (whether or not he is identical with the author of the original) commits an error of fact, but they can, unfortunately, never be rendered "right." I defy anybody to give me the full English equivalent of such simple and frequent German words as "*zart*" or "*echt,*" or, conversely, the full German equivalent of "big" (as opposed to "large" and "great") or "shocking."

In evaluating a translation we have, therefore, to refrain from squabbling over single words or even sentences. What can be rendered more or less adequately is—barring factual mistakes—the linguistic personality of the work and not its verbal elements.

Taking this for granted, I was greatly surprised by Mr. Gannett's criticism. I had greatly enjoyed Mrs. Lowe-Porter's translation because it manages to bring to mind—or, rather, to ear—the very flavor, the very cadence and inflection of Thomas Mann's German while not attempting to stick to his words; I actually heard the German sentences while reading the English ones, not in spite of, but because of the fact that the elements were not "identical" in the sense of the Dictionary. In sum, the experience was not unlike that of a good portrait which may evoke the personality, the gestures and even the speech of a man, not in spite of but because of the fact that the curve of his nose, in terms of a mathematical formula, differs from that which is seen in the picture. Thus I could hardly understand how this translation could be called "wretched" until I discoverd that Mr. Gannett contrasts Mrs. Lowe-Porter's "stuffy and awkwardly Victorian" translation with Thomas Mann's "easy-flowing and colloquial German." I am not expert enough to say whether or not the translation is "stuffy and awkwardly Victorian." But I do claim the right to assert that Thomas Mann's German is not "easy-flowing and colloquial." His prose is, to quote from the description of his idealized self-portrait, Mr. Aschenbach, *"erlesen,"* that is to say, it is choice, deliberately literary, stylized and at times purposely archaic. It has, in other words, precisely those qualities which, with a negative accent, may be called "stuffy" as well as "Victorian." He loves to use words with "overtones," and when the subject is delicate, he uses, purposely and with great artistic effectiveness, such obsolete words as *"libertinisch"* or, conversely, such archaically coarse words as *"Vettel"* in order to create a distance between the thing expressed and himself; he touches the object with gloves, as it were, to make the reader see how clean his hands are and how dirty the object is, and his wardrobe, metaphorically speaking, contains both white kid-gloves and tough gardening gloves. His grammar, too, is now deliberately Early Nineteenth-Century, now parodistically businesslike, now crisp and supercilious, now, quite deliberately, faithfully "first grade."

I feel that all these qualities, such as they are, come out in the translation as clearly as humanly possible, and that— whatever the merits of Mrs. Lowe-Porter's work from the point of view of English prose—Mr. Gannett's criticism is based upon a fundamental misunderstanding of Thomas Mann prose. Of all epithets which could be applied to his German none seem to me less appropriate than "easy-flowing" and "colloquial."

Judith Heller had this to say about it:

Reading *The Beloved Returns* with the German version side by side, I find that this is by no means a literal translation. The original has those long sentences, a somewhat artificial 18th century atmosphere, which the English has only in spots, though it does come through in the dialogue. In Mann's German there is often a subtle irony, expressed through the German particles *"noch, doch, mal."* The somewhat stilted speech of the humorous character is good in English. Altogether the fabric of the English is so well-woven that one does not feel the German through it, which is, after all, what Helen wanted it to be. Where there is a shade of meaning in the German, it is reproduced in the English, not always with the same part of speech, sometimes in a succeeding sentence.

The translation of *Lotte in Weimar* as *The Beloved Returns* was published in the ominous year 1939, and in 1940 Mrs. Lowe was working on the short trifle *Die Vertauschten Köpfe*, which was translated as *The Transposed Heads*, although Mann would have preferred *Heads and Bodies*. In May and June, while Mann was writing about problems of translation, Holland, Belgium, and France were crumbling beneath the Nazi onslaught, and Mann wrote that he found "it difficult, almost impossible, to give these matters any thought at the moment, nor to busy others with them," but he was practical enough to state that "these English editions are my one and only standby, for surely my writings will never again appear in German as long as I live, and perhaps never again in France." These lines were written on June 20, 1940, when France had been overrun by Nazi troops.

"I am writing without special reason for it, just to write you and because I have the feeling that we should hear

from one another again," Mann wrote to Mrs. Lowe on
May 24, 1941. "I hope that you and your excellent scholar
are well in your attractive new home. We frequently
remind each other of the friendly and entertaining fare-
well evening there [in Princeton]. Since then much time
has gone by, much has been experienced. Much has
happened and many new events have piled up." He was
right: 1940 had marked the nadir of the fortunes of the
democracies. Within the year the Battle of Britain had
been won; the United States had traded a hundred destroy-
ers to England and had just extended the first peace-time
draft in history. The Manns had moved to Southern
California, where they were building a house. His letter
continues:

We are living temporarily in a pleasant, rustically situated
small house near the ocean. At the beginning, after the
complicated journey, interrupted by lecture-stops, I was beset
by a dental crisis and was in some pain. But now, with the
help of an excellent Hollywood dentist, a new period of peace
has set in, which will hopefully last till my blessed end. This
might possibly be far removed—for an insurance doctor who
recently examined me found me so very healthy that the
company mercifully will be ready to accept me as an insurance risk in spite of the almost completed 66 years of life. I
seem to myself to have been cheating but it might be that the
climate of California provides the insurance company with a
guarantee against loss. This definitely agrees with me—the
assurance that every day will be dry and fine is a great
advantage—and the final volume of *Joseph* progresses in spite
of many interruptions by "worldly" matters which here, too,
claim attention. At the moment I am working on the important conversation between Joseph and the Pharaoh Amenho-
tep, leading to the promotion of the former. This is the critical

scéne à faire—after that I am out of the deep water. Knopf has already sent me several copies of *The Transposed Heads* (*Heads and Bodies* would have been better, I think). You too will have received some of them and will surely agree with me that the book is very nicely gotten up. I am particularly pleased with the large good type which I consider an honorable testimonial to your translation—my German version was not treated so well. Unfortunately there is the danger that in these troubled times the book will be completely ignored—something I would hate to see—no less for the sake of the precious earnings.

Our plans for building—these, as well as the very intention to build—have undergone many ups and downs. It was in reality we who vacillated, not surprising in these times. We had already decided to abandon the whole matter, compensate the architect for his trouble and retreat. But now it seems rather that we will begin to build anyway. I believe that the matter appears more dangerous than it actually is. If you rent a house now, it had better be done for a long period of time, because rents will surely increase. So, why not do this in the way of paying off a Federal loan-rent—which is less than what we would now have to pay for a rented house satisfying our requirements. Forgive these ruminations—Joseph becomes the man of business in the current volume.

"Your letter touched me," Mrs. Lowe replied on May 30, 1941, "and gave me much pleasure, though some sense of guilt as well, for I had meant to write myself and had not done so." After agreeing that it was an unfortunate time for the publishing of *The Transposed Heads,* she added: "I do not know if I ever yet properly expressed the profound sympathy I have for you in your predicament of having to have a translator! I am almost certain that I should dislike anybody who made me a changeling child, a wooden doll in the cradle, instead of my living flesh. I don't mean that I now feel the translations are wooden; but that I should almost certainly feel so in your place. It is good that you contrive to forgive me."

Meantime, Mrs. Lowe had been asked by Bruno Frank to translate his novel *Die Tochter,* and on July 18, 1941, Mann wrote anxiously from Pacific Palisades, California:

. . . I surely would not want to be in your way with my affairs when you are attracted by an interesting task. But I was just on the point of sending you the beginning of *Joseph the Provider,* hoping that you would be able to begin gradually with the translation. What is ready for you in typescript is only part of what I have written. The book is making fairly good progress and it would be fine if the translation could keep pace with the work on it. In this manner we would both finish about the same time and both the original and the translation would be ready for publication simultaneously. Nevertheless there is still much to be done on it; a whole little world of story-telling still lies ahead of me and I must still reckon with a whole year before it will be finished. Nor is there any guarantee for that. It might even happen that you would soon have stolen a march on me with your translation and would have to wait for more material. That might cause you to regret having given up the other interesting job for the sake of the *Joseph.* It is very hard for me to judge whether you would be able to attend to both jobs at the same time or alternately. I cannot possibly ask you to devote yourself exclusively to the *Joseph* which is *"une mer à boire"* and that you keep yourself free for it. But what about the volume of essays? Would that not give you work to do as well? And how much time would the job take up that you have in mind? [9]

[9] Mrs. Lowe did not translate the Frank novel and was consequently able to devote her energies exclusively to Mann's work.

We are glad to hear that you are so content where you are located. The climate here is attractive but wearing. Blood pressure decreases, the thyroid gland functions less well, it makes one tired, slack and stupid. My animal spirits have been somewhat improved by the doctor's prescriptions. We have bound ourselves for better or worse to this enchanted mount of Venus. The Seven Palms House rises above the ground. But we can sell it soon again.

On March 7, 1942, Thomas and Katia Mann were examined as future American citizens,[1] and a recapitulation of Mann's political and social development seemed advisable in this crucial year of the war into which the United States had just been drawn. "There is more hope now than ever before," Frau Mann wrote to Mrs. Lowe on November 11, "the days of the monster draw to a close." Mann had been thinking of a collection of his literary essays, which Mrs. Lowe had started translating. On April 17, 1942, he wrote her:

I turned over the problem of the essay volume in my mind for a long time and arrived at the conclusion that a volume such as we had planned, a volume containing all my literary essays, at the moment not only would have no effect, but also not the least success. I cannot imagine that more than one or two dozen people would show any interest under present conditions in topics such as Amphitrion, Platen and Storm, or even in Schopenhauer and Goethe. To publish now would mean missing the right moment. On the other hand, a volume of moderate size confining itself to the political category would be assured of a certain measure of attention. I was not surprised to find Knopf agreeing with me.

[1] The Manns were sworn in as American citizens on January 5, 1944, by coincidence the date of publication of *Joseph the Provider*.

While they were corresponding about the projected volume of literary essays Mann made another venture in criticizing the English translation of one of his favorite essays:

I am anxious about the first long essay, "Sufferings and Greatness of Richard Wagner." This is one of my favorite pieces, treating a subject very close to my heart, a subject by its nature highly problematic. Accordingly, it is dealt with in a very subtle way, a manner which the psychoanalysts would call "ambivalent." I could scarcely imagine a more difficult task for a translator, and I am sometimes uncertain whether originally the translation at first venture was a complete success. At the time when the English version appeared, I received a number of letters in which the writers complained that the English text left several things unclear. My request, which you will understand, is that when you prepare the volume of essays you look over this piece again, compare your translation with the original and do me the favor of seeing that every sentence has the most adequate rendering. I should be most grateful if you did this.

Order of the Day contained his political essays and speeches of two decades, from "The German Republic" (1923) to "Niemöller" (1941). In the Foreword he made generous amends to those who had talked of his "aristocratic retirement" from all but German problems, insisting, however, that he had been conscious of and explicit about world problems in such works as "Fiorenza," "Death in Venice," "Mario and the Magician"—above all in *The Magic Mountain*. Any lingering doubts about his "aristocratic" position were dispelled by "This Peace," written after the betrayal of Czechoslovakia to Hitler in 1938: "To be against such a thing as Hitler is always to be right, let it turn out as it will," he asserted. "The way that history has taken in this instance is so foul, it has such a stench of lying and knavery that no man need be ashamed of having refused to accept it." Earlier having defended the position that Germany, "the Heartland," could supply the synthesis between the excesses of the despotic East and the equally deplorable excesses of the social-democratic West, Mann now came forward as a fervid but perhaps insufficiently prepared convert to "The Coming Victory of Democracy," as he phrased it for enthusiastic audiences in his adopted country.

Perhaps Mann's enthusiasm overran his political knowledge—or so, at least, Mrs. Lowe believed. "I am just finishing a volume of his political speeches and letters for press," she wrote to an intimate friend, Mrs. N. K. Wells, in July 1942: "Does great credit to his heart and powers of eloquence and knowledge of Germany, but far behind in information and knowledge about our side. Too bad. Nothing can replace reading. He has such a good heart, such an eloquent voice, such a large audience; I do wish he knew more. I am meditating telling him so."

We may assume that she did not "tell him so," but she did try to fill him in with her own "Letters to the Editor" and with references to apt political treatises. In July 1942, when she was working over the material for *Order of the Day*, she wrote to Mann to compliment him on:

the high purpose, good vision and clear common sense of the "Appeal to Reason." And so when I read your Foreword to this volume, I was glad to find in it the words ". . . its essential purpose was to make the German citizen understand that if German freedom and world peace were anyhow to be saved, his political station in the struggle was by the side of the workingman. A bourgeois-socialist alliance, a compromise between democracy and socialism, which today the whole world sees as the indispensable condition of future well-being and the price of victory in the present war, might at that moment have saved Germany and the world from catastrophe. But the idea was only sentimental raving, doomed to be drowned out by peals of mocking laughter."

This is a concrete program, and germane now to this country and the Allied Nations, as it was to Germany at the time when you wrote it. It is what I have been saying for years to everybody who would listen, and wishing I had an audience. I wrote an appeal, in this sense, to Churchill, in reply to his broadcast to this country soon after Munich. But, it could not, under the conditions, be broadcast; and in my search for an organ I let it fall into the hands of kind people who thought it was a little too strong, so nothing came of it. What Churchill said on another occasion is so bitterly true: "When you leave the region of platitudes you enter the realm of the controversial." Platitudes are always true, and they are easy to write; but unfortunately, by definition, they have already become meaningless. And any concrete program is bound to reveal the split which exists inside of every nation. You wrote that you always read *The Nation;* so you must have seen Del Vayo's fine article in the issue of June 20th. Here is its 3d paragraph, in case you do not have it by you: "This puts in a nutshell the disastrous connection between diplomacy and the prevailing economic system. I wish I happened to have here as clear and brief a statement of the corresponding link between the middle-class position and that same economic system: the confusion which causes the middle classes to concede whatever concessions must be made must never compromise the basis of the present social system."

In 1940, it was the Labor vote which outweighed the votes

of the middle and upper classes and elected Roosevelt. Of course there were many votes for Roosevelt from both of the two latter classes as well; most of those people are entitled to be called the "intelligentsia," in a serious sense, since they took a long and an objective view even of their own interests. I sincerely feel that these people now have an important duty, in the sense expressed in the words I quoted from your "*appel.*" Misgivings about Labor, in this country, anybody is entitled to have: it has not passed through the disciplinary and maturing experiences of Labor in the European countries, especially England. Still, in the present situation, I think we are able to feel certain where Labor will stand in the next Presidential election: it will stand for war to a finish and for changes in the economic structure. We are not entitled to feel any such security about the middle classes. This electorate, probably more than European ones, is subject to fatigue of attention; to relapse into "normalcy"—in fact if we can judge from the past, it would not be at all hard for vested interests to bring such a mood about once more, when the alternative looks like a discouraging succession of years in which our material prosperity and standards are being battered to pieces. Few besides students of economics and history will grasp that the causality is in the reverse direction and that it is the economic debacle which is cast in the role of cause.

In less than two years we shall be in the midst of the ballyhoo of the nominating conventions for the Presidency. But two years is quite a long time, and much can be done in it. In passing: it took only two years to swing this country from 100% anti-war to 100% (nearly) pro-war. A fact. In fact, much is being done now: the radical and liberal press, columnists, radio and all sorts of groups and societies are doing wonders; and under the sheer pressure of events [as] psychologists say, even more might. But it is still true that the press, almost as the French press was, though by a much more complicated and indirect process, continues, as it was, probably 80% anti-New Deal, though now, perforce, 100% pro-war. Here we have the "split," statistically expressed. To make the middle classes aware of it, aware of the connection between war and the social structure, is a task of the first importance, already being worked on by many fine minds. But here I am reminded of something Professor Einstein said to me when I was telling him what an opportunity he has, because people so greatly respect his opinion: "Yes, yes, they like me when I say what they want to hear, but not when I don't." Conscious and purposeful antagonism and counter-offensive, of course there will be. But pessimism aside, it is a great thing to have a concrete program: and you will tell me if you have seen anywhere persistently enunciated this program of yours, for I have not. Whereas it might be like a slogan, like *écrasez l'infâme*—only constructive, not destructive. A slogan is a spur to the emotions, but here we have also such irrefutable arguments few ears open to reason. Both are needed. And who will apply them? There are many brilliant constructive minds still not being bent upon the task which is so vital. I am thinking in particular of the academic world, prone to be "sicklied o'er," etc. A great many of them *see,* yet feel that their world is a world apart, what the collapse of that world would be. They are a little like your picture of yourself before 1914. Or do you think it is better like this?

Please forgive me if this letter finds you in the midst of other preoccupations. It can be put aside and not answered at once. But up here—at sea, as it were—in the profound quiet and the bracing air, and the complete absence of "engagements," I find my mind dwelling on these subjects. I hope you are all having a good and satisfactory summer—insofar as one can. Best wishes to everybody.

In reply Mann wrote on August 2, 1942:

You have written me such a nice, long, clever, political letter which arrived just at the right time. I was ill in bed with an intestinal grippe for a few days and could make good use of reading matter. I need scarcely tell you that your thoughts echo mine—and this is not surprising, since they follow closely one of my ideas expressed at an earlier date but always adhered to since then. This is a thought that undeniably has swayed and moved men and even active statesmen ever since I expressed it in that "Appeal to Reason." That is, if the statesmen can be trusted. Vice-President Wallace—surely one who can be trusted—has pronounced the slogan you asked for in his speech. His concept of this war as a people's war, a war for the people and their freedom, a war ushering in and laying the foundations of the century of the "common man" agrees with your and my view. And later, when Sumner Welles spoke in similar terms and disavowed the capitalistic imperialism of the 19th century—even though his real personal convictions seem somewhat more doubtful—we could witness to what historic pressure the statesmen of today are subjected. They cannot speak otherwise than they do.

However, the question remains open whether the promises exacted under the stress of war will be fulfilled after the victory has been won, helped on by these promises. I fear the comparison is obvious with the promises given the Germans during the struggles against Napoleon. These wars of liberation were not permitted after the victory to be called anything but "wars of deliverance," with deliverance merely applied to foreign dominion.

Our anxieties, no less than our hopes, are centered on this country. Our great hopes are aroused by its mighty physical strength, its gigantic industrial ability that can be put forth for the war effort, virility and youthfulness of its population, its soundness, its great potentiality to believe in the good, in improvement. Anxiety is caused by its political naïveté [*Unerwe-*

cktheit], its persistent lack of understanding what it is all about, what is at stake. I have just had some correspondence with Hendrik van Loon, whose nephew and brother-in-law were killed by the Nazis in Holland. He wrote me: "You are right, a thousand times right, we are paying for our past sins, but the men who were most of all guilty of those sins are still in command and until they shall have been removed we shall continue to suffer defeat. I am sorry that I cannot speak with any pride of the role our country has played thus far in the struggle. We, or rather Washington has completely failed to mobilize the civilian population. America is not in this war; its purpose is, its heart is not. The boys are doing their duty and doing it with great courage, but they have no notion, no idea whatsoever what the shooting is all about." And further on: "Our sluggish democracy will have to become an effective democracy with a definite mission of its own or perish."

All this is very true and agrees with your views. One has the feeling that in order to be able to carry on this war with overriding belief and enthusiasm America would first have to pass through a revolution. But there is no time left for that, and this is the dilemma. In spite of this, even in England, fighting for its life, something has come about which might well be called a social revolution. The twenty-year alliance with Russia seems to me to be a fact possibly having historic significance for humanity.

As I said in one of the essays: Let us hope that this alliance enforced by the necessities of war between Russian socialism and Anglo-Saxon democracy may have great and propitious consequences in the future.

Viewing it as a whole, I do not consider it too sanguine or utopian to believe that, impelled onward by the present crisis, humanity is actively taking a big step forward and rising to a higher level of social maturity.

Of course this takes for granted the elimination of the

present German government and a complete revolution in my country which will sweep away those layers of society who stood for the nationalistic, bellicose and reactionary ideas.

Again thanks for your detailed arguments revealing so clearly the well-being of leisure and the fresh sea winds. In the meantime your later note about the preface and the changes made therein has arrived. I am greatly relieved by the friendly welcome you give to my proposed corrections. I think Miss [Freda] Kirchwey should be informed of them; she wrote me very kindly about the preface and wants to publish it, only slightly shortened, in the second part.

To reciprocate for the charming picture of your grand-daughter, I enclose a small photograph of our little grandson, Fridolin, who is again staying with us for a few weeks.

Do take care of yourself and have a good summer. A new portion of the Joseph manuscript will follow soon.

Your devoted,

T.M.

Thomas Mann had indeed come a long way from the cultural isolation of 1918, when he had attacked his brother Heinrich's attachment to Western European democracy and socialism. It is a typical Mann irony that in 1947, according to Katia Mann, Heinrich's daughter could say to Erika Mann: "Your father is far more radical than mine!"

The years in Princeton were happy ones for Mrs. Lowe as she approached her seventieth year. She and Dr. Lowe built a house on the grounds of the Institute for Advanced Study, where they entertained the Manns, the German-American authors Hermann Broch and Bruno Frank, for both of whom she did some translating, the historian Erich von Kahler, Erwin Panofsky, the mathematician Hermann Weyl, and the economist Winfield Rieffler, who was their next-door neighbor. There was a constant flow of émigrés from war-torn Europe, many of whom she was able to help with money or employment. Her oldest daughter, Prue Smedts, was living with them while bearing *her* oldest daughter; her youngest daughter, Patsy, was in nearby New York. Albert Einstein, a professor at the Institute, became a particularly close friend; he would stop by the Lowe home on his way from the Institute to his house on Mercer Street. Mrs. Lowe gladly translated many of his letters, papers, and addresses. His letter to Mrs. Roosevelt commiserating with her on the death of her husband reads in Helen Lowe's English like prose poetry.[2] This friendship meant a great deal to Mrs. Lowe, for their ideas on racial minorities, on race relations, on pacifism, and on the importance of the work of Sigmund Freud, were strongly akin.[3] Einstein served as godfather to the little Dutch

[2] *Sie haben den grössten Verlust erlitten, der einen Sterblichen treffen kann. Mit Ihnen trauern die Menschen aller Länder, die ehrlichen Willens sind und den Glauben an einer bessere Zukunft sich bewahrt haben. Er führte, ohne dass die Geführten der Illusion ihres selbständigen Handelns beraubt wurden. Das Bewusstsein, dass Sie mit Hingebung und Erfolg ihm in seinem Werke zur Seite gestanden sind, wird Ihnen ein Trost sein in Ihrem grossen Schmerz.*

You have suffered the greatest loss that can befall a mortal. The peoples of all lands grieve with you: all men grieve who are of good will and who have preserved and cherished the belief in a better future. He led, without depriving those who followed of their sense of responsible choice. The consciousness that you stood devotedly and effectively at his side will console you in your great sorrow.

[3] Their ideas on radical economics coincided, as this letter written in German by Einstein on August 28, 1945, just after the A-bomb had devastated Hiroshima and Nagasaki, indicates:

As you well know, I share your opinion, indeed, I may even express it more radically. I am convinced that it is extremely harmful if private interests are involved in the armament business. It seems to me quite self-evident that this state of affairs has to be stopped for the sake of the development of international politics.

daughter born in Princeton to Prue Smedts, whose husband was serving in the Dutch resistance. Although an avowed and ardent pacifist, Mrs. Lowe, like Thomas Mann, permitted herself no doubts about the war against

---

But, beyond that, I am also convinced that the production of all industrial goods by private enterprise makes it impossible to solve in a reasonable way the problems of the distribution [division?] of labor. It is the natural tendency of the profit system to decrease the number of employees and workers, thereby reducing the purchasing power and, indeed, the economic security of the majority of the population.

Keeping scientific knowledge of military importance a national secret will inevitably lead to new wars. These will be preventive wars started by those countries who believe themselves to be temporarily ahead of others. I do not put much stock in the ability of scientists to prevent this evil since they are caught in a kind of wage slavery and since there will always be enough among them to break through the ethical cordon. The only solution is organization on a supranational legal and executive basis. There is a strong movement afoot to influence public opinion in this direction. "Mr. Swing from Washington" also works well and effectively for this cause. More when I see you.

Kindest regards to all of you,

Ihr Albert Einstein

The Lowe-Einstein relationship assumed the proportions of a partnership, as this little poem shows:

TO A. EINSTEIN
On a Modest Occasion

The record of this partnership unequal
Shall now be duly banked;
Yet not before in fit and proper sequel
The gentle donor's thanked.

Sweet unction to the Lowely accessary
This piece of paper lays;
In gratitude wherefore she would not tarry,
And in requital prays:

If it be not too wilfully aspiring
That she such hope espouse—
Then, lion, roar, when next you are requiring
And she will be your mouse.

Nazism, which was being supported by one son-in-law in the Dutch resistance, by another in the English navy, and by a number of her younger friends in the United States army, in which Klaus Mann was now also serving.

After the publication of *Order of the Day* in 1942, she was working on the translation of the fourth and last volume of the Joseph series, *Joseph the Provider,* which appeared in 1944. For relief, perhaps, from the daily stint of eight hours on the Mann books, Mrs. Lowe turned to work of her own—mainly on political and social topics— letters to the editor, essays, and miscellaneous notes. And she wrote her first play, *Abdication.* For years she had been reading the Chronicle Plays of Shakespeare, and when, in 1936, Edward VIII was forced to abdicate the throne of England, she adapted the sorry histories of Richard II, the three Henrys, and their successors to the personal tragedy of Edward, doomed to a life of obscure exile with his twice-divorced wife.

"The imitation, such as it is," she wrote in her foreword, "in style and structure, of the Chronicle Plays was undertaken in order to produce the effect of historical continuity with the Shakespeare plays." It was an act of daring to challenge Shakespeare on his own ground, with Edward dallying with his divorced lover, parrying his mother, the Dowager Queen, defending his marriage to the woman he loved against the moral mouthings of the Prime Minister and the Archbishop of Canterbury. So she gave the Bard a chance to talk back in the Epilogue about "this upstart crow [who] hath sought to beautify herself with my feathers, and [who] hath bombasted out some lines of blank verse." But Shakespeare craved "indulgence for this poor play, for what are these kings, these princes and dukes, these folk both gentle and simple? What but history? And what is history? A chronicle. And what's a chronicle but Time? 'Tis a setting down of Time's passing, with such passing embellishments as may arrest that bald sexton to make us mindful of him."

In these words Mrs. Lowe shows how she shared with Mann a preoccupation with Time as a basic constituent of human life. Every reader of Mann must be impressed by his use of Time as a sort of fifth dimension—in *The Magic Mountain*, in the Joseph series, in *Doctor Faustus*. Mrs. Lowe had worked out ideas of Time on her own, and in her essay on *Doctor Faustus* she "timidly advanced" the idea "that the involutions of the time dimension employed as a technique by modern novelists . . . may represent approximations of our shifting point of view with respect to the element of time." Time, she asserted, will enable man to survive, even to progress, and such she suggested was the message of *Doctor Faustus*:

There hope, the instinctive awareness, is not for men but for man—the hope that humanity as such will through time once again resolve the tragic defeats of religion, politics and art which are incidental to the rationalization (in the older sense) of new knowledge out-topping knowledge; since that today has burst our frame and made us retreat disorderly into an anti-humanistic phase as we labor after some viable synthesis of knowledge and faith.

The play *Abdication*, or *All Is True*, which employed these considerations of Time, was offered by the Dublin Gate Theatre Company in Dublin on September 28, 1948, and was hailed as "first-rate theatre" and as "something more than a clever piece writing to deal with new British political happenings . . . behind a very slender Elizabethan disguise." It was, *The New York Times* reviewer concluded, "a fast-moving, kaleidoscopic historical pageantry in the grand manner." It is reported that Billy Rose, impresario of the best of the new and of the old adapted to the new, saw the play, liked it, and asked if he might turn it into a musical for the New York stage. Mrs. Lowe indignantly refused. But *Abdication* was published by Alfred Knopf in a beautiful edition with photographs of the actors and of some of the scenes, as "a poetic drama of the young king who preferred the woman of his choice to the throne."

The play was still searching for a producer when, on July 9, 1943, Mann wrote the author:

I came to ask myself whether I had told you how much I liked it for its natural Shakespearean manner, the way it showed up the historic unity, the eternal, timeless Being of the English world. There is a kind of dreamlike charm in giving a modern event this historical form in which it is as convincingly English as anything that can be found in *King John* or in *Henry IV*. Such an impression is heightened as your adroit, unerring, easily spoken verses, without any affectation whatsoever, transform this newspaper story of yesterday into a poetic, dramatic episode.

When the play had been produced and published, Lion Feuchtwanger added his note of praise on September 25, 1950:

I have read *Abdication* with redoubled interest, because I was held not only by the subject and its treatment, but because of the stylistic experiment it represents: a personal problem to the author of historical novels. Besides, I once collaborated with Bertol Brecht on a very freely treated version of Marlowe's *Edward II*, performed in the Berlin State Theatre.

Your method of viewing important historical events as it were from a distance, seems to me to be particularly successful. The somewhat playful, purely artificial aspect which characterizes less important episodes by using this method, does not detract from the play itself, but gives it a special flavor.

Meanwhile, the writing and translation of *Joseph the Provider*, last of the four volumes, was proceeding apace. "I am touched by your zeal and industry in working on this translation and regret only that the task gives you some trouble," Mann wrote on June 18, 1942.

I hope to be able to advise you on some details, but as far as the verses are concerned, I am compelled to admit failure, as my English sensibility is not sufficiently developed.[4] Personally I should be best satisfied if the translation followed as closely as possible the rhythm, rhyme and vocabulary of the original. The shorter verses have a Goethe-like and romantic cadence, but in between the rhymed verses, some longer doggerels with scarcely defined rhythm often approach the movement of the psalms and use their vocabulary.

Goethe was one of Mann's chief influences, and Goethe had projected a poetical work on the Joseph theme. Here again, Mrs. Lowe shared Mann's reverence, writing about the Goethe lectures that Mann delivered when he first came to Princeton:

In these lectures T.M. quoted much Goethe, and I remember how much I enjoyed putting the delightful, simple, genial verse, with its feminine endings, into English. I have been, only in my own mind of course, conceited enough to fancy

[4] Although for twenty years they had corresponded each in his own language, in 1941 Mann began to write some short letters in English. This one is still in German, like all the longer ones.

that I could make a good new English version of *Faust* Part I! Of course, I have not the necessary scholarship! I must here, I feel, confess with shame that I sometimes do not "really understand" T. Mann until I have undressed his thought and put an English garb on it.

Seldom before had Mann offered suggestions to his English translator, but his own English had so improved that he felt able to interfere. On July 16, 1942, he wrote:

Sincere thanks for sending me your excellent translation of the preface [to *Order of the Day*]. I am always afraid that it must appear not only pedantic but tactless as well to approach a translator like yourself with counter-proposals. But I well know your kindness and your devoted interest in seeing to it that everything is reproduced in English most adequately. And so I take the liberty to meddle a bit and to trespass on your territory. Wherever you consider my proposals to be mere bungling and do not believe that you can be answerable for them, you must of course ignore them completely.

How Mrs. Lowe answered we do not know, but she did write to Alfred Knopf on July 16, 1942: "Though he is usually justified in his negative comment, the positive suggestions he makes are not English and cannot be used."

"It is only a matter of a few passages," Mann had written, and the changes he suggested were indeed minuscule. "The Lowe writes well but slowly," he had written to his son Klaus, but he had never tried to hurry her until 1943, when Alfred Knopf wished to announce *Joseph the Provider* for fall publication. Thinking perhaps of his only regular source of income, Mann wrote delicately on February 26:

I know full well and so does Knopf that it is almost brutal to hurry or even to spur on a translator like you. Nevertheless I

85

cannot refrain from making the above friendly request, with the proviso, of course, that what you do must conform to the standards which you yourself have set for your work. Do not take this insistence amiss, and give me a word of comfort, if possible.

Mrs. Lowe evidently uttered the "word of comfort," for on March 17 he wrote: "I almost reproach myself for having urged you on. I am fully convinced that you are doing your best in every way." And on April 29 he added:

I have read with the greatest pleasure your translation of the little scene "Israel stands before Pharaoh." It seems to me that the pages have been translated as masterfully as the Thamar chapter, and if the whole volume turns out that way, all of us —Knopf, you, I and the readers—can be very happy.

You will forgive me if I am impatient to see further samples of your translation in advance, also for the reason that I might still give you a corrective suggestion here or there. Would you be so kind therefore as to send me some parts of the translation which you consider ready for publication? I should take care of looking them over as soon as possible.

This letter was written by Mann in English, to one word of which, "masterfully," Mrs. Lowe dryly added in her own hand: "He means masterly. But that word is falling out of usage in U.S.A. 'Masterful' only means strong-willed."

As Mrs. Lowe raced (if that term may be used about her meticulous method) toward the fall deadline, Mann grew really excited. On June 26 he wrote:

I have now read those parts of the *Joseph* that you have sent me and have been delighted with them. I do not believe that I shall have to take exception to more than a few items . . . my feeling is that you have done excellent, one may say

unexcellable, work. Everything flows along simply and naturally, and I almost have the impression that in English the
Pharaoh portion is less difficult for the reader than in the
original German. It remains a tax on his patience in any form.

In the prelude, I could not, try as I would, find anything to
note except for a doubtful phrase at the bottom of the first
page: The German passage refers to the First Book of Moses,
Chapter 19, verses 4–8. It should be translated approximately
as follows: "When an unspeakable duty (or something similar) had been exacted from two of us." This is all as far as the
Introduction is concerned.

In the Pharaoh chapter I noted nothing except that small
but crucial difficulty of rendering in English the difference
between *"am Himmel"* and *"im Himmel."* I have underlined
the words "my father in Heaven" wherever they occur in the
manuscript because I, thoughtlessly, did not anticipate this
difficulty and only became aware of it at the place where
Pharaoh, aided by Joseph, recognizes that he must say *"mein
Vater im Himmel"* and you left a blank in your translation. We
must find a way out of this dilemma. It is impossible to have
Pharaoh say from the start "my father in Heaven," for this
state "in heaven" is only discovered later. Nor is the adjective
"heavenly" possible—since this refers to a spiritual not a
spatial heaven—the firmament, the skies. I believe we shall be
reduced to having Pharaoh speak, during the greater part of
the conversation, of "my father on the firmament—in the
skies," for what he implies is the sun itself, from which the
father ostensibly was descended. "My father in heaven" should
not appear before page 212, where Pharaoh is reminded that
"mein Vater am Himmel" is wrong and should be *"mein Vater
im Himmel."*

Joseph the Provider did not meet the fall deadline, but
was published in January 1944. It must have been a great
relief to the author, to the translator, and to the publisher

when the last volume of this mammoth, 1,207-page novel was off the presses and in the hands of the reading public. Bruno Frank sent Mrs. Lowe this supreme accolade on July 17, 1944:

Let me congratulate you on the completion of the translation of the Joseph tetralogy. Thomas Mann has read aloud to us the greater part of *The Provider* in the course of recent years; as a whole story I know the volume only in your translation. And I am again quite moved by the great measure of faithful rendering, devotion and splendid achievement it exhibits. You have so signally made the impossible possible that one is moved by gratitude and deepest respect. How happy our friend must be to have found you so early in his career and that you have accompanied him all along his triumphant way!

And for you it must be a happy feeling too (I believe) to look back on the endless tremendous pains you took with this task. You have achieved something that will stand the test of time. For your translation will remain the sole translation into the most important world language as long as Thomas Mann's work will last. Your name will be linked to his for all time. There are translators whose name endures. No one now reads the writings of Schlegel or of Tieck, but every German associates their names with *Hamlet* and with *Othello*. You have assured for yourself an immortality; to know this must be good. We insignificant "originals"—99/100 of all writers—cannot say as much for ourselves.

In typical fashion, Mann relaxed by writing a short coda to the *Joseph*, *Tables of the Law*, which Mrs. Lowe translated, even though Mann had promised "not to burden you with it." On March 17, 1943, he wrote:

I was stimulated to write this postlude to the *Joseph* by the plan for a collection of short stories relating to the Ten

Commandments. At first I was to write the preface, but now the result is this story. It was written quickly and easily, as it were for pleasure. It is customary that after having completed a major piece of work I permit myself such a diversion: after *The Magic Mountain* it was *Disorder and Early Sorrow;* after *The Beloved Returns* I wrote very quickly *The Transposed Heads.*

The story deals with human morals, and after many light passages it ends with a very stern and severe curse placed on him who persuades men to abjure moral values.[5]

While the final volume of *Joseph* was rolling through the presses, the indefatigable Thomas Mann was at work on a novel which was to be the climax of his life work— *Doctor Faustus.* "While still in Pacific Palisades," he wrote from Boston on December 22, 1943, "I tried several times to tell you something about the new novel, but something intervened every time."

When the war reached its climax in the Allied invasion of Normandy on June 6, 1944, Mann had written 220 pages of "the new novel," which he had not yet named. Some problem about the choice of a translator had engaged both Mann and Alfred Knopf, but they both stood firmly behind Helen Lowe, and on May 1, 1944, Mann wrote in unconcealed relief:

I am very happy about this solution. . . . Intelligence and ambition are not enough. The lack of all poetic qualities, particularly the sense of humor, was only too apparent to me [in the other translator]. I can tranquilly and gratefully give my consent [to your translation] because the matter of translation still appears to me as something quite unreal,

[5] The reader may well be reminded that in the short pronoun "him," Mann was deliberately referring to Adolf Hitler.

purely theoretical. The experiment is so hazardous, the execution so difficult, the whole enterprise so far-reaching, so limitless, that translation appears to me as a matter for "after the war"—in other words, for a moment the advent of which is beyond belief. And yet this moment will come, if enough time is given me. Nor can I tell you how comforting the thought is to me that in the future the task will again be in your hands. I cannot thank you enough for your steady loyalty to all my endeavors. I know well enough how great a share your art of interpretation had in securing the good fortunes of books like *The Magic Mountain* and the fourfold *Joseph* in this country.

Although I am already on page 220 of the new novel, I have not wanted to think of having a typescript, for there is much in it about which I do not yet even know whether it will remain or not. However, just before your letter arrived I had given my secretary some pages to copy and if there is enough on hand, I shall send you several chapters so that you may at least make some contact with the book. I think I can still send them to Princeton.

Naturally the use of an English dictionary will be important for some exact translation. But you will also need a German dictionary, an odd, archaic one. It is a strange thing about this book; though its action takes place in the present, it always has a trace of the 16th century in Germany; it has, so to speak, one foot in the time of the Reformation.

How great are the tensions under which we live! The most tremendous, most daring military undertaking is imposed upon the most peace-loving, least militaristic nation! Klaus is in Italy, Golo in London, whither Erika, now in uniform, is about to go again.

Germany made him think of Faustus, and Faustus made him think of Germany, a Germany under the demonic spell of Hitler, a Germany which had sold its soul to the devil, not for creation, but only for destruction. Like Doctor Faustus, syphilis-ridden and sliding down the inclined plane which could lead only to hell, Germany in 1944 was fast sliding to defeat and semi-annihilation. "Germany will probably soon be at the end of the tether," Mann accurately predicted on June 2, four days before the Normandy invasion. "Yet the era of wars and revolutions in which we are living will hardly come to an end and can persist even without Germany. I am quite content that during my life span not many more of these 'entertainments' will occur." Earlier in this letter he noted:

Now our *Joseph* has come out and I have seen a number of reviews. Some were poor and stupid, others better. Above all, I am happy that in this instance at least, with the gigantic work completed, your tremendous achievement is evaluated with fitting respect. I hear that *Time* magazine wants to publish your picture.[6] I have told you recently how aware I am myself of the debt of gratitude I owe you.

In *The Story of a Novel*, Mann's only "book" about one of his novels—an indication of how important he considered it—he talks of how, in 1943, he grasped the "central idea: the flight from the difficulties of the cultural crisis into the pact with the devil, the craving of a proud mind, threatened with sterility, for an unblocking of inhibitions at any cost, and the parallel between pernicious euphoria ending in collapse with the nationalistic frenzy of Fascism" (p. 30).

"The loyal translator," Mann also noted in *The Story of a Novel*, "for the most part so reticent from sheer modesty before the work entrusted to her, sent a letter: 'I strongly feel,' she wrote, 'that in this book you will have given your

[6] *Time* did, on July 17, 1944.

utmost to the German people.'" Mann had paid an indirect compliment to Mrs. Lowe in the Epilogue to *Doctor Faustus*, where he has Serenus Zeitblom consider the impossibility of publishing a record like this in Germany during World War II:

In actual fact I have sometimes pondered ways and means of sending these pages to America in order that they might first be laid before the public in an English translation. . . . True, there comes the thought of the essentially foreign impression my book must make in that cultural climate and coupled with it the dismaying prospect that its translation into English must turn out, at least in some all too radically German parts, to be an impossibility.

This Epilogue and the Translator's Note were written, of course, long after the inception of *Doctor Faustus*, which took four years to complete. Mann faced such tremendous difficulties in composition, correction and further correction that he felt obliged to write on June 2, 1944: "My various announcements that I shall send you the new novel for your perusal are almost becoming ridiculous. . . . But I assure you that some day when you least expect it the intricate, queer thing will arrive." In the latter part of 1944, when the Allies were pounding Germany into submission, Mann, who kept on writing and revising, finally sent on part of the *Doctor Faustus* manuscript, explaining in a letter of January 20, 1945:

I fully shared your uncomfortable feeling that we had lost touch with one another. But I was not a bit better off than you. I too was quite ill at times, a bad influenza struck me down in late autumn and it persisted in the form of a trigeminal inflammation. I am still suffering from the aftermath of that, and the nervous system seems to be still affected by that attack. Nevertheless I continued to work most of the time but had to restrict my correspondence. I lacked the determination to send you more manuscript. But now I shall really do so, and the manuscript will follow soon upon this letter. The reason I kept on delaying from the very first, and again and again, was that I was always wishing to add something to it that would give you a more complete picture.[7]

I heard with pleasure that you have already begun work on the translation. Do go on translating without further concern the parts which interest you—for these are surely all right and will remain. But I should warn you against translating everything I send in succession. I distinctly feel that when once the whole lies completed before me, I shall go over it with a red pencil and eliminate much that is spun out and tedious. I mean the theoretical musical passages which might well lack liveliness; I would not like to have you take pains with them for nothing. You will not risk doing this in the purely narrative parts.

In a more familiar tone he added:

We could almost envy you for your wintry snow flurries. Yet here our winter too is exceptionally beautiful. We are at the moment being compensated for a cool and foggy summer by warm sun and blue skies that have continued like this for months.

Our Christmas was really quite according to the tradition— a children's festival. We had our four grandchildren with us, the two small boys of our youngest son from San Francisco, and the two little girls of the Borgese couple together with

[7] "Dr. Kahler tells me T.M. is sweating blood over the new novel," Mrs. Lowe had written to Mr. Knopf on March 1, 1944. "Its theme is—as I seem to understand—the political aspect of the romantic movement, in a musical setting. That would certainly be a bit difficult to translate." Little could she guess just how difficult it was to be!

their respective parents. At the moment Erika is here with us, back from Europe, where she naturally had many interesting experiences. She told us about Paris, Brussels, Antwerp and Aix-la-Chapelle. She immediately gave a series of lectures here on the West Coast and she is leaving now for three months to keep her other engagements in the Middle West and the East. We hope that she can spend May with us. At the end of May we want to travel Eastward together. . . .

Do take care of yourself, dear friend. Katia joins me in cordial greetings. I hope that the impending manuscript will find favor in your eyes.

While he was writing and Mrs. Lowe translating *Doctor Faustus,* two incidents temporarily clouded the friendly professional relationship between the two. Knowing little about American journalistic practice, Mann sometimes blurted out injudicious or unconsidered statements to reporters. When in 1944 an interview with a *Time* correspondent left the unfortunate impression that Mann was not satisfied with his translator, Mann immediately set the issue straight in a letter (*Time,* July 17, 1944):

It is my wish to take the opportunity to prove my gratefulness to my translator of many years, Mrs. Helen Lowe-Porter, for the extraordinary achievement she has accomplished with the translation of all my books, from *Buddenbrooks* up to the last volume of the Joseph series. I am fully aware of the tremendous difficulties which my not exactly simple way of writing puts in the way of her mediatorial zeal and faithfulness, and I cannot appreciate enough the great credit Mrs. Lowe-Porter has earned with her linguistic reproduction of my work for the English-speaking public. Not always have the reviews done her full justice, and that is why I wish to express my appreciation publicly. My literary standing in this country and in Great Britain would certainly not be what, gratifyingly, it is if I had not had the good fortune of finding a translator of the devotion and linguistic talent of Mrs. Helen Lowe-Porter.

Unfortunately, less than a year later, the same misunderstanding arose about Mrs. Lowe's translating abilities. In an interview with Frank Harriott of *PM*, Mann said: "To translate artistic prose into another language is as difficult as to translate poetry." The newspaper seized on this as an indication of Mann's lack of confidence in his translator. Not so, replied Mann:

. . . I am sure that when Mr. Harriott and I were speaking about the difficulties of translating literary works from the original language into another, I did not omit to mention the extraordinarily fortunate situation in which I personally happen to find myself. Indeed, I have repeatedly expressed on many an occasion my thankfulness and satisfaction for the good luck that has allowed me to entrust my books to the care of an exceptional translator, Mrs. Helen Lowe-Porter. Her gift of tongues is as philologically conscientious as it is artistically inspired, and without her help it would have been impossible for my books to reach audiences as relevant and as favorably disposed as those to which Mrs. Lowe-Porter conveyed with such passionate brilliance their intentions and meanings.

Mann followed this public commendation with a private one to Mrs. Lowe on July 19, 1945: "I can never pronounce too much praise in public for all you have been doing in behalf of my work. Knopf . . . is greatly attached to you and will remain loyal to you . . ." Before she received this expression of confidence from Mann, Mrs. Lowe had written to Alfred Knopf about the contretemps: "You may have got from T.M. a quaint account of what really happened about the *PM* interview. I found out. It seems that T.M.'s credit in my family and among

Princeton friends is not higher than mine in N.Y. What annoys them is that he always acts as though I were not there, unless I am called to his attention—a fine masculine attitude for which—I dare say—I am partly to blame."

Mann-Lowe relations were bound to be strained from time to time, but the friendship remained firm to the end. There was some trouble in 1944, when Mrs. Lowe wrote to Alfred Knopf on April 24 that "I do not blame T.M. at all for finding me a bit difficult. . . . I do think he is a really great person. I love and revere T.M.'s mind, and think he is a good as well as great man; if he understands this, it is all that is necessary."

After talking about the "new novel" for over a year, it was not until September 28, 1945, that Mann could write: "I shall soon send you a large portion of the new *Faustus* manuscript. . . . I am at last on page 500, which is about two thirds of the whole. How frightful! This too is again a *'mer à boire,'* a deep receptacle with room for too much— Germany, the era, art, everything. Why did I ever meddle again with such matters?"

Earlier in 1945, on February 18, he had written about the labor involved:

Now, while I am at work on the novel which is so inexpressibly difficult, I almost envy myself for that period when, relieved of the *Joseph,* I improvised *Tables of the Law* with a kind of elation. I often think, with melancholy, of the verses from *Love's Labour's Lost:*

> *There form confounded makes most form in mirth*
> *When great things labouring perish in their birth.*

These lines surely had their origin in some personal experience, even though they may not apply to their author. *Faustus* following upon Moses makes me think of this. It is a "great thing labouring," and sometimes I have doubts whether, from a purely sporting point of view, I am still capable of meeting the demands it makes. Though I admit that an element of excitement, which was part of the plan for the book, still has its constant effect. In the end event, the subject of the book is Germany. You will have remarked that and as you continue to read it will notice it more and more.

The allusion to *Love's Labour's Lost* he explained in a letter of October 8, 1945:

That Adrian is attracted to *Love's Labour's Lost* is due in the first place to the element of parody in it; for it is really a satire on humanistic preciosity. Shakespeare took aim at culture because he was not a cultivated man and was despised for his lack of an academic education. I can well understand that this is why he depicted culture in its most ridiculous aspect.

Toward the end of this letter he confided: "Sometimes it seems to me that I ought to rewrite the whole thing. But perhaps this idea is a form of hypochondria." Fortunately for himself and for his translator, he did not indulge his literary hypochondria.

Perhaps this explanation helped Mrs. Lowe, who had been puzzled by the first 261 pages of the novel. She had written to Alfred Knopf on August 28, 1944: "I do not yet know what he is driving at, and this first part, written in the first person by a pedantic, middle-aged scholar, is not calculated to stimulate interest—certainly not in style and hardly so in subject matter. Which is a pity, because I assume that there is going to be quite a lot about Nazi-Germany with a new and unhackneyed approach. . . . The musical matter is v. interesting."

"The task of rendering the *Faustus* in English was a

very difficult one," Mrs. Lowe declared, in a miracle of understatement, in "On Translating Thomas Mann." "I was incompetent to make anything satisfactory of the great musical erudition displayed by the author and was obliged to get help from a competent musicologist." In order to get into the mood, she took a recording of Beethoven's piano sonata in C minor, Opus 111, to her Maine island. "But I am still extremely dissatisfied with my version of the words which Dr. Mann sets to the second movement of the sonata," she added, speaking of the *"Lebewohl"* section on pages 53–6 of the translation. In May of 1947 she wrote a progress report to Mr. Knopf:

The work, *Doctor Faustus,* is, in the German text, 959 pp. long. I have finished the first draft of the whole and the typing of it is nearly done. Various chapters have also been revised and could be copied. But the bulk of the difficulties has still to be dealt with. I found a capital man (a musicologist attached to the BBC, a Viennese [8]) to help me with musical parts, which are extensive and complex. I do not anticipate any more difficulties on that score. I have also now found an Oxford don, a Mediaevalist, who out of interest is willing to help me deal with the vocabulary of Reformation German, which has to be put into suggestively archaic theological English without being in any way local—no small job and I could not do it in many months without his help. No wonder T.M. felt vaguely uneasy: no one but a Mediaevalist could do it, and the author is in great luck that one has been found. I am leaving for Holland on May 19th, and I expect to be there all summer. My English secretary will join me there, and the ms. will get copied as fast as the difficulties are dealt with, chapter by chapter. I wish I could say when it will get done, but I cannot tell. . . .

[8] Dr. Mosco Carner.

I should like to say a few more words about the book: it is, in the first place, as T.M. says himself, so very German that no English can do it justice and nobody but Germans can v. much appreciate it. The translation will get v. many hard knocks. It is written in unadorned prose, not beautiful, without pretensions to style—this again T.M. told me himself. It is gauche; it would benefit by drastic cuts; it is not simpatico—even less than usual. In part it is a turning-out of his memories for many years, some of them trivial.—But it is massive, like everything else he does. And it is, in absolute truth, a *modern* Faust. Did you never feel reading Goethe's or Marlowe's, that the hero was making a bad bargain, that you could not imagine what he did in the way of dissipation which was in the least worth what he paid? Dr. Mann made this point in his lectures on Goethe's *Faust,* and he at least does not make this mistake. What his hero got is worth the price; it is the immense joy of creation, creation in the realm of music. The human brain cannot imagine anything higher or better. In another way also it is modern: in its treatment of the supernatural. You are left not knowing whether anything daemonic really came about or not: an attitude of open-minded scepticism towards the supernatural, a partway yielding to the possibilities, which I think is characteristic of the times.—My musicologist says that every musician will read the book with the greatest interest: on that side it is a picture of disintegration, in passages of much theoretic fascination. And Germany too—the hero dies in 1940, and the narrative continues up till 1945—Germany too goes mad and dies. You see. There is no hope anywhere, save the hope *jenseits* [beyond] despair, of which he rather vaguely talks at the end. Some people will skim through the book to see what sort of picture is made of the "decent" German in Nazi times. But it is too hard a job; I do not find the professor a convincing character.

Like many readers of *Doctor Faustus*, Mrs. Lowe was not completely satisfied with the work as a whole. "It is a pity the great book," she wrote to Mr. Knopf on January 6, 1947, "—I mean I think it is great—is so uneven, magnificent in parts, in parts still old-fashioned, with human beings cramped into the Procrustean bed of his grand cosmology. The book is really a parallel with the *Zauberberg:* what that book did to sum up the epoch of the First World War, this one does for that of the Second." This thought she expanded in her unpublished article "Doctor Faustus," agreeing with Ludwig Lewisohn that *The Magic Mountain* "was a novel written with the full intellectual equipment of the first quarter of the twentieth century."

And now: to write with the full intellectual equipment of this second quarter of the same century, this dazed, disequilibrated, disintegrating, yet pregnant time; to state it, to give it contour and content with the tools of intellect and art—since I, at least, feel that such was again the author's function—was that in any way possible?

It is considered to be the office of great art both to utter and to interpret the age. It may seem to do this with immediacy or over a period of time; the effect is achieved in both ways. And the statement appears to apply to each one separately, of what we call, collectively, the "arts." The question then is: could a single novel—as it were, a *Don Quixote* of a novel—possibly perform the feat of expressing and interpreting the second quarter of the twentieth century? I submit that the answer is affirmative.

To prove her point, Mrs. Lowe wrote twenty-seven typewritten pages of analysis and criticism of *Doctor Faustus,* perhaps the best interpretation of this great synthesis of the life of Germany vis à vis the world during and after Hitler. She took fourteen pages to prove that "Dr. Mann draws an explicit parallel between his hero's demoniacally inspired music and the anti-democratic, anti-humanistic philosophy which was taking shape in Europe and which resulted, in Germany, in the Nazi regime." Earlier she warned that "there is a risk that many readers may take the novel as applicable merely to the German nation and people. I am concerned that the universality of the critique be pointed out; that we should be aware that the bell tolls for us too." Or, as she put it in her Translator's Note:

. . . this *monstrum aller Romane* is addressed not only to Germans, not only to Europeans, but equally to ourselves. All that our world has lived through in this past quarter-century has forced us to enter this climate and to recognize that these are our proper stresses. Readers of *Faustus* will and must be involved, with shudders, in all three strands of the book: the German scene from within and its broader, its universal origins; the depiction of an art not German alone but vital to our whole civilization; music as one instance of the arts and the state in which the arts find themselves today; and, finally, the invocation of the demonic. It is necessary for us to read *Faustus*, even in a version which cannot lay claim to being beautiful, though in every intent it is deeply faithful.

In her first draft of the Translator's Note, Mrs. Lowe had so stressed the difficulties of the novel that Mann and Knopf were alarmed lest her warning drive off potential readers and buyers: "I am infinitely sorry that you are being bothered by the request to make changes in the quite properly framed 'Translator's Note,' " Mann wrote on April 1, 1948.

From its beginning it was very good and clever. I felt only a bit anxious—and Knopf shared this feeling with me—that in its first draft it described the novel too emphatically as a difficult, high-brow book. But it would have been sufficient simply to have omitted "only for intellectuals" and left the rest, which was very good.

After this comment upon the possible economic repercussions of labeling a novel "For intellectuals only," Mann launched into a rare author-translator debate:

. . . The third draft sent to me by Blanche [Knopf] struck me as a bit meager in its second paragraph. That I interpreted the first quarter of the century in *The Magic Mountain,* the second quarter in the *Faustus,* sounded to me too much like a prosaic program. The reference to *The Magic Mountain* is intrinsically correct; *Faustus* does continue in the same direction—a criticism of current circumstances—but does this in a much more intensely poetic, more passionate, more emotionally upsetting way. In the episode of the exorcism of the devil there is mirrored the all-embracing crisis of our era; its pangs are accounted for in the novel by a spiritual summing-up. The fact that the novel takes the form of a memoir is so because this is not only its outward garb but the essential pattern for it. It is a tale describing life with uncompromising, almost savage directness. It transcends literary values; it is something new and final seen in the light of my other works—perhaps in the light of contemporary literary production anywhere. If it was worth while, in fact imperative, to undertake the extraordinary difficulties of making a translation, this is so because it is a thoroughly international work in interpreting the present state of Western culture. It is this in spite of the fact that it is extremely German in its outward aspect, deals agonizingly with German character and German fate and is linguistically rooted in the German past. Its internationalism is the explanation why it has been received with strong emotion on the Continent, in Switzerland, in Scandinavia, in France, and even in Germany, as no other book of mine has been received.

Of course, a Translator's Note must not indulge too much in critical praise of the object. But if you wish to state why the reading of this book is indispensable, you might perhaps find something to complete the second paragraph in the passages written above.

Nevertheless, I shall be satisfied if you should find that what I have written goes too far and feel that we had better keep your short formulations.

Mrs. Lowe altered the second paragraph, and Mann welcomed the final version of her Translator's Note, commenting that "your translation will resemble the picture of a woman who is not only beautiful but faithful as well" (April 19, 1948). This comment echoed the opening of her Translator's Note, where she quoted:

Les traductions sont comme les femmes: lorsqu'elles sont belles, elles ne sont pas fidèles, et lorsqu'elles sont fidèles, elles ne sont pas belles. From a more familiar source we are instructed that "to have honesty coupled to beauty is to have honey a sauce to sugar." And on the highest authority of all we know that the price of a virtuous woman, with no mention of other charm, is above rubies. All things considered, what remains to hope is only that the English version of *Doctor Faustus* here presented may at least not conjure up the picture of a *femme ni belle ni fidèle.*

Three years of writing and translation (1945–48) had preceded this compliment to the translator. "What an imposition to have it translated," Mann wrote on August 4, 1946. "It is an impossible task, of which I am fully aware. You ought to hate me for having been born and being such

a nuisance!" Just the fact of its being "an impossible task"
challenged Mrs. Lowe, who had read the original version
before Mann made his many cuts. "Your previous reading
of it has given you sufficient insight into its meaning and
intent," he wrote on August 29. "You will have noted that
its organization is not 'according to motif,' as it is in the
Joseph and in *The Magic Mountain*." After warning her of
the difficulty of rendering Old High German into modern
English, he concluded:

And now, good luck! You will be busy enough with this
portion for a time. I shall send some more soon. While you go
into battle, I am trying busily and with some success to get on
with the last part of the novel. Sometimes I think of dividing
the whole work into "books" to facilitate a more lucid view of
the whole. [This he did not do.]

My best wishes for your health! For selfish reasons, I now
care about that no less than I do for my own!

In 1946 Mrs. Lowe had given up the Princeton house
and moved with her eldest daughter to London, whence
she wrote on September 3:

Conditions here are difficult, in many ways; but I think I
shall be able to settle down comfortably with nothing to do
except work. . . . Now for the *Faustus*. I am not surprised—
or rather, I shall not be—if you have misgivings. If I do the
work, I shall of course work regularly and steadily, and at
nothing else. But of course I cannot now—any more than I
ever could—say that I shall do so many pages a day and by a
simple multiplication give you a date of delivery. You know it
is not that kind of work—at least not for me.

"It is hard to state what you will have accomplished
once this task is finished," he replied on November 7. "My

French translator . . . has, as I am told, given up before
starting, because she does not believe herself capable of
making an adequate translation of the *Faustus*. You see
what a brave woman you are!" On December 20, 1947, she
wrote to Alfred Knopf:

Here is what I actually wrote to T.M.: In answer to the part
of your letter telling me how brave I am, I do think I ought to
say that I undertook this piece of work with fear and
trembling and actually did refuse it but finally yielded to
Alfred's blandishments.[9] This does not alter my conviction
that if I had time—say another six months—I could make a
really good job of it.

You see, with the word perfect—which is of course nonsense—we get back to the problem which has always troubled
us. The job is to some extent an artist job, and I have always
felt, with the more difficult books, that I should work over
them without a thought of a time limit. But that is not the
market or the publishing house view of translation. If it is not
perfect then it is bad. I do not know how to deal with these
blacks and whites, for my mind deals in delicate shades of
grey. To be serious: I simply cannot afford to spend another
six months on this job, much as I should like to.

Some indication of the difficulties of translating *Doctor
Faustus* are revealed in this letter of November 7, 1947:
"After having worked at it for three years, I wrote the last
lines of the *Faustus* yesterday," Mann wrote triumphantly
on January 31, 1947. "Thirteen chapters plus an epilogue

[9] Another indication of the confidence that Alfred and Blanche Knopf
placed on Helen Lowe's translating abilities is shown in a Mann letter of
August 20, 1948: "Knopf would like to have a new translation of the
Dostoevski essay from you for a volume that is to be called *The Thomas
Mann Reader*. It has been translated already by someone else, but Alfred
believes that you are the only one to do it. Will you please, therefore,
start work on it and send the manuscript directly to Knopf."

will be added to the manuscript which is already in your hands. A fine kettle of fish! Yet it could not be made shorter. . . . To bring such a piece of work to a conclusion might be viewed as a considerable moral victory. Whether anything else of importance has resulted from such labor must be left to the verdict of one who plays such an important role in the book."

During the three years of writing and translation, their relationship warmed from a "Liebe Frau Lowe" to "Liebe Freundin," and then to "Dear Helen," while he became "Dear Tommy" to her. In 1946 Mann had been rereading the anniversary issue of *Neue Rundschau*, a *Festschrift* for his sixtieth birthday in 1935, when he wrote to her that he "read again the wise and warm words which were your contribution to it." In her article, "The Thought, the Word, and the Deed," which refers us to Faust's considerations of the proper translation of *Logos*, "In the beginning was the word," the opening lines of the Gospel of St. John, Mrs. Lowe used a quotation from *Tales of Jacob* as epigraph: "It was this disposition to mental association which governed Jacob's spiritual life, to the extent that it actually created the form of that inner life, and his thinking was almost completely concerned with such associations."

Even as Jacob's garments were fringed and full-fashioned, so also were his thoughts. In his musings, one thing always led to another, he dwelt above all upon the connections between ideas, as did his son Joseph, in fact (though with a difference, for he was a man of action); as did good Hans Castorp, in his unassuming way (who was a man of no action at all); as also does the creator of these. He, too, in all his "stories" is bent on this one thing: to link up and combine, to adumbrate a picture of a whole. Here lies the province of all those who, like Jacob, are "played upon by chords and correspondences"; who move in a world of chiaroscuro, of yes-and-then-again-no and one thing endlessly melting into another; of deeply entangled fringes of feeling and thought, of shifting associations and combinations, no shadowless brilliance of atomic exactitude. Such power of evoking the racial unconscious will always be found combining what is hard to combine and yet what *has need to be combined*. It is possible that here lies the explanation of Thomas Mann's popular success, in the face of this scholar-artist's bulk and weight of erudition, in the face of a style so conditioned, as style should be, by its content, that it can by no means be read while running. Probably we are in great present need of his services. Where not alone the average today but the very sagest stand staggered at their inability to combine the mutually annihilating elements of our civilization into any imaginable pattern; now it is we have need of such an artist, weaving the garment of his time for us to see it by. For first our morbid state takes comfort, as like from like, in this art, it addresses itself soothingly to our ails. But after that we are led on, we take lessons in the art of combining, we seek sanity in the persistent effort to relate all things to the whole. Not the artist, of course, nor we, nor any coming age, will ever succeed. The task must ever be done anew; yet precisely today we have a grievous need to be at work on it.

It may make an odd impression, when one whose concern has so explicitly been with this writer's words, dwells so particularly upon his thoughts. But the antithesis, of course, is a false one. For to the artist word and thought are like body and mind and cannot be divorced. Indeed, no one so well as the translator can estimate the affront dealt to this artist by our time, in that his works must be known so largely in other tongues than his. Finally, in these few lines of tribute it is

scarcely upon the Word as Thought that the writer of them
would lay stress. Rather she would be at pains to condemn
another divorce, equally unfortunate, which takes place in our
common thinking when we make an antithesis between words
and actions. For now, today, in our present anguishes, surely
we may, appraising Thomas Mann's work, speak of the Word
not alone as Thought but even more cogently and inevitably as
Deed.

"I fear that I have never thanked you for [these words]
explicitly," Mann added. "Let me assure you that I was
deeply moved by the homage shown in these lines by my
translator. And at a second and third reading this feeling
returned in all its strength."

Mrs. Lowe completed the translation of *Doctor Faustus*
early in 1948, and the English version was ready for the
market. Mann, whose living depended largely on the
royalties from the American editions of his books, wrote to
her: "Let us hope that the Book-of-the-Month Club will let
the book appear in November, otherwise we would have to
wait until 1949, which would be hard. But how dare one
quarrel and argue with a deity? Our countenance must
never lose the expression of meek rapture."

Happily, the Book-of-the-Month choice for November was *Doctor Faustus* (a dual selection with a slight
Maugham book), and Mann exulted on September 14,
1948:

How good must the translation be to have received such
enthusiastic reports on it from the Club's readers! The news
that, in addition to all the pains that you have taken about the
book, you have also written an article on it surprises and
moves me. To have the woman who knows the novel as no one

else does, every word and every secret corner of it, write about it will be exciting and affecting reading for me.

After reading the English version and complimenting Alfred Knopf "on the excellent appearance of the volume," he wrote to Mrs. Lowe on October 3, 1948:

Now I have the urge to thank you once again—this time after direct examination and study—for this tremendous and faithful achievement of interpretation. I do this most solemnly and sincerely. Your doubts, expressed in your ingenious short introduction, whether the translation is beautiful as well as faithful, I consider unjustified. I am not on sufficiently good terms with the English language to be entitled to express praise, but I have read much in the volume and have found that the translation reads like an original, like an English prose work. This implies that you have known how to find equivalents in English for the German, which often employed strange expressions, and have understood how to strike the balance between the anomalies of language. This, as I see it, has reconciled beauty and exactness.

You did quite right in allowing the German word to stand in several cases. There is one place where you did not do this, though it would really have been relevant there: I mean in the Fitelberg chapter in which the guest speaks of Anatole France and makes the joke that a German writer could not call himself "Deutschland," he would have to call himself "Deutsch," and that would be a Jewish name. Here "Deutschland" and "Deutsch" should have been used, for "Deutsch" is a well-known Jewish family name, while "German" has no meaning in this context. A German man-of-war is of course called "Deutschland" not "Germany." This should be changed as soon as possible. Do forgive this small criticism of an achievement which is so admirable as a whole! Now let us see

how the American critics and the American public will deal
with the novel. If they reject it—it will not be your fault.

Mann did not need to worry about public reception of
his novel; the first edition of 25,000 was exhausted in the
first month after publication. Always a keen businessman
like his burgher forefathers, he anticipated a good sale of
the British edition, and he believed Mrs. Lowe's article on
Doctor Faustus "would do much to pave the way over there,"
as he wrote in English on January 8, 1949:

Now your Faustus-article is in my hands and with it the
comment of the most thorough and intimate connoisseur of
the book. You may believe me that I have read your study with
keen interest and great satisfaction. Every line bespeaks your
loving absorption into this work, and above all the article
shows you as the thoughtful sociologist and socialist that you
are. I haven't yet read a review of the book demonstrating
such great receptiveness for its socially critical feeling, for the
presentiment of the *end* prevailing in it and for the ominous
trembling of the foundations which it transmits to the reader.
Your article is an admirable supplement and consummation
of your achievement as a translator. It is, of course, highly
desirable that it reach a broad public. The American press is
probably too satiated with more or less uninspired reviews of
the book. But in the spring, I believe in March, the novel will
be published in England, and I should very much wish that
your article could be printed in an English periodical. It would
do much to pave the way for the *Faustus* over there.

In her essay on *Doctor Faustus,* with the epigraph from
Blake: "The road of excess leads to the palace of Wisdom,"
Mrs. Lowe states first: "It is considered to be the office
of great art both to utter and to interpret its age." Its
theme, "the invocation of the demonic," was no less

apposite for the sixteenth-century philosopher than it was for twentieth-century Germany. "For Dr. Mann's purposes Adrian Leverkühn (Bold Liver) [1] had to be sceptical and superstitious; passionate and frigid; an artist and a scholar; provincial and cosmopolitan. As all these things together he could stand for 'Faustian Man' "—like Germany in the twentieth century. Serenus Zeitblom and Adrian, "hero and hero-worshipper, are a deliberate, at times almost forced confrontation of the humanistic and anti-human," the two faces of modern Germany. "As complementary figures they recall—of course with differences—other such contrasts in Dr. Mann's novels: Tonio Kröger and Hans Hansen; Hans Castorp and Joachim Ziemssen; Naphta, Settembrini and Pieter Peeperkorn, etc. Indeed, Dr. Mann and—Dr. Mann. And all of them with variations present the conflict between the lawless and the disciplined within the personality of the artist." Adrian, as bourgeois and composer of music, "is unique, a genius; but at the same time he and his art can only represent his age of disintegrating norms and ironic gropings."

After briefly summarizing the plot, "as though the work were a novel like another," Mrs. Lowe launches into her interpretation, asking first: "Can any single work of art command the full intellectual equipment of our day? Could it weave for us the garment we see our time by? *Doctor Faustus* deals with a German genius, with the German nation and with an art which, though like all great art, universal, is yet in a sense a peculiarly German art. . . . I am concerned that the universality of the

---

[1] Miss Ida Herz noted that "Mann composed the name, as I know from himself, from '*kühnes Leben*'—'bold life.' "

critique be pointed out; that we should be aware that the bell tolls for us too." After analyzing the musical-demonism of Leverkühn, Mrs. Lowe concludes that "Dr. Mann draws an explicit parallel between his hero's demoniacally inspired music and the anti-democratic, anti-humanistic philosophy which was taking shape in Europe and which resulted, in Germany, in the Nazi regime." Commenting upon "the sententious remark of the Evil One in Chapter XXV: 'Reality? Is not reality what works?' Here we have the philosophy of Nazism, pragmatism gone mad."

After discussing the "dehumanization of art" in the modern world, Mrs. Lowe suggests that "no one could read *Doctor Faustus* without realizing that in it the 'hot' problems of our time of troubles are very definitely being raised. These *are* the things we talk about, the things we feel. The novel crushingly responds to our sense that our world today is at the season of mourning; that we must not seem to scant the present of its dreadful due, but in season fitly and duly mourn, and that art expressive of our state will be the issue of our woe—as in the Gothic time the wry and wailing mouth of the Mother of Sorrows expressed the age's overwhelming sense of sin." She spells out, by quotation from various musical and literary philosophers, the despairing modern *Weltanschauung* (ca. 1948—the beginning of the Cold War). "Demonology, the demonic; irrationalism; anti-humanism, dehumanization. To 'pick up words as pigeon's peas,' these are the ones we hear and see bandied today, with assent or with dissent. They express a distrust of humanity and human reason."

In these words Mrs. Lowe plucks out the inner meaning of Mann's message—the decadence, the deliquescence, the downfall of Western liberal and intellectual civilization. It was a practical irony that Mann, the prophet of pathology, who had defended imperial Germany in 1918 against the Western democratic tendencies of his brother Heinrich, should now resolve his personal dilemma of expatriation by attacking the demonic possession of Germany—the Heartland of civilization, as it had seemed to him in the first quarter of the twentieth century.

Mrs. Lowe's article may be interpreted as a cynical interpretation of a pessimistic analysis of the modern world. Is there no hope for humanity in the modern world? There is none for Adrian at the very end: "This dark tone-poem permits up to the very end no consolation, appeasement, transfiguration," Mrs. Lowe concludes.

Hope is explicitly denied to Adrian, his nation, his art. And to us? It is no part of Dr. Mann's thesis to enlarge upon such a hope, but only to raise it. Perhaps the figure he made his own, the figure of the revolving sphere, taken from Egyptian mythology, is here comfortingly in place. There hope, the instinctive awareness, is not for men but for man! The hope that humanity as such will through time once again resolve the tragic defeats of religion, politics and art which are incident to the rationalization (in the older sense) of new knowledge out-topping knowledge; since that today has burst our frame and made us retreat disorderly into an anti-humanistic phase as we labor after some viable synthesis of knowledge and faith.

The reception of *Doctor Faustus* by the reviewers was discouraging to Mann, who complained to Mrs. Lowe on January 8, 1949, that "the American press is probably too satiated with more or less uninspired reviews of the book." But the review of Harry Levin, professor of comparative literature at Harvard, had savagely attacked the translation on the grounds of the "archaic English, inaccuracies in choice of English equivalents," and, triumphantly, of the omission of several passages in the German original. Mrs. Lowe wrote to Mr. Knopf, answering in detail all charges:

Herewith at last a few comments on Dr. Harry Levin's review of *Doctor Faustus*. And first about the omissions to which he refers: about two weeks before the finished English version went to the publishers, Dr. Mann sent to me a list of certain passages to be omitted. Pages 91–94 of the German text were on the list and I suppose that this is the three-page cut to which the reviewer refers although I have not the English version by me to compare. There are a good many other cuts; I do not know whether or not they were to be taken out of the German version as well. There is a paragraph in the review comparing cursorily *Doctor Faustus* with *Jean Christophe*. It is somewhat revealing; and it is indeed interesting to see how a man can comment upon himself in the choice of a single word. I mean the word "chatty," surely both pejorative and peevish. If Dr. Levin were applying it to our humanistic pedagogue the word would be in place, since after all our Serenus is a character in a novel and he *is* chatty. But Dr. Levin is clearly applying it to the author of the book, who I would contend, never is, in any usable sense of the word. Its use says more about Dr. Levin than it does about Dr. Mann. The same comment is applicable to what the reviewer says about the archaic English employed. I assume that he has the scholar's point of view. If so it is odd he will not recognize that "ye olde tea-shoppe" did not originate in some spinsterish nineteenth century brain. "Shoppe" is current fourteenth to seventeenth century spelling, and "ye" a survival of a then obsolete symbol for "th." As for "gode boke" the problem is rather more complicated. Both "gode" and "boke" are spellings current, among others, from the fourteenth to the sixteenth century. But in the absence of all my notes I cannot be sure where I got this term for the Bible. I suspect Tindale, as I used him and the Tindale-More controversy a good deal, as well as Wiclif and Coverdale. I think "Holy Writ" might have been nicer, but I do not know its pedigree either. As for *Dunkelmänner*, according to the Cambridge Modern History, this group of scholars is referred to in English as "The Poets." It might have been nice to put in parenthesis "The Obscure Men" like a textbook. In general one may guess that in the chapters using archaic language Dr. Mann, like Homer, "went and took what he thought he might require"—"the same as me"—and did not hew to the line about centuries. It would be quite impossible to *translate* in any literal or scholarly sense those chapters of *Doctor Faustus* where Lutheran or sixteenth century orthography and vocabulary are used. On this point I consulted three mediaevalists, two English and one German, and we decided that it would be an impossible plan to take a German word or expression and find its equivalent in English of the same period. It would in many cases simply not exist or for one reason or another be unavailable. I used the principle of substitution, which I believe to be both valid and necessary in translating a work of imagination, though scholarship would always look askance. Of course in using it one must never avail oneself of anything but the author's own style. On the other hand a result based on scholarly principles would produce a wooden piece of work, boring to read and unfaithful to the creative imagination of the author. I conceive that the author might prefer his translator to be faithful to his creative imagination, but I may be wrong; I know many people believe that translation is *per se* an *Unding* [chimera].

The above notes are all comments upon specific points in Dr. Levin's review. I think they should not comprise as well a general criticism of a critique. I would however like to suggest that perhaps Dr. Levin arrives at the meat of the matter only in his last paragraph. There he compares Mann's *Faustus* with Goethe's, and it seems vaguely to occur to him that Dr. Mann's novel, if one may call it that, harks back *with intention* to the earlier pattern—only because, as the reviewer says, "we have lost touch with enlightenment and humanitarianism." Once more, to quote Ludwig Lewisohn's comment on *The Magic Mountain,* Dr. Mann has written a book with the full intellectual equipment of the second quarter of the twentieth century, an achievement which Dr. Levin, as it were, praises "arsyversy." But in Lessing's words "was würde Goethe *itzt* sagen?"

A copy of this she sent to Mann, who replied on January 8, 1949:

I have never seen this review, but I have heard plenty about it. His chief complaint about your translation seems to concern certain differences between the German and the English edition, namely the omissions in the English one, which he blames on you. As you say, it is, of course, a fact that I made these abbreviations myself in order to facilitate the translator's job. I decided to do so when my French translator declined the translation for fear that she would not be able to do justice to the technical-musical passages. I consequently struck out several paragraphs of this nature—not only for her but for all translators, and it is possible that at the same time a few other things of non-musical content fell by the wayside.[2]

But it is strange that Mr. Levin should deplore this relatively small loss. Surely he ought to be glad that such a bad book is shortened by a few pages.

[2] In a letter (written in English) of August 16, 1946, Mann noted: "I keep asking myself whether or not certain abridgements of passages which are hardly accessible to a non-German public, are indicated in the English edition of the book. That, too, is a problem which moves me to retain the manuscript for a while yet."

Before *Doctor Faustus,* Mann had gathered together all the literary essays by which he desired to be judged; these were published as *Essays of Three Decades* in 1947. "The volume of essays is about done," Mrs. Lowe wrote to Mann from Oxford on July 17, 1946: "It seemed a simple bit of work, but there were many variants in the text, due, I suppose, to editing—I had in effect to do the whole German text over again, 700 pp."

"I often think of all the trouble you are having with my essays," he answered on August 4, modestly adding: "Nobody will ever read the book—it is only for the record." Then he reported on an operation he had undergone in Chicago: "I am recovering quite well from my clinical adventure; only an immense scar going from the chest to the back reminds me of it. They opened me up quite extensively and even removed one of the ribs. I suffered it all with great good nature."

In most of the essays she ran the German quotations with an adjoining English version. The poetry of Chamisso, Platen, and Storm she let stand in German, with a translation in the appendix. In a charming but modest Translator's Note, she explained:

In Storm's case the simple, highly evocative charm does not, so to speak, stand export well. Like certain fine wines its aroma evaporates. On the other hand, the inclusion of the originals enables the reader of the verses with very little German to evoke their peculiar music by reading them aloud; the prose version at the back will give him their content. As for Platen, it seemed force to embark upon a technical imitation; so the same plan was followed with Storm.

In the letter of July 17 she enclosed a little engraving of Zürich "found by me in a collection made by some member of my family a hundred years ago, when he made the 'grand tour.'" For she knew how dearly the Manns loved Zürich, that most German outpost in Switzerland, where the Manns were finally to settle. On August 16, 1946, Mann acknowledged the gift in English:

I can thank you only very shortly for the charming little engraving you were kind enough to send me, and again and again I regard with admiration. I am also showing it with pride to friends of the house, and just a few days ago, Bruno Walter occupied himself with it for a long time.

It would seem that Mrs. Lowe must have sent another picture, for on February 28, 1947, Mann wrote: "The day before yesterday we received your kind present, the charming view of Zürich; my wife and I were delighted by it. The picture arrives at a moment when we have some hope and the prospect of seeing the good town of Zürich and our friends there at an early date. We are still not quite certain whether this journey can be realized because of the great difficulties of transportation; and we still receive warnings about the generally chaotic conditions in Europe."

The relationship between Mrs. Lowe and the Manns (Frau Mann was her husband's alter ego in all matters) was by no means limited exclusively to literary affairs. We have seen how in 1937 Mrs. Lowe had tried to convince Mann that "the struggle is not between nations but between forces within each nation"—a clear Marxian interpretation of history. When she was translating *Order of the Day*, Mann's political and social essays, she regretted that he was "far behind in information and knowledge about our side." In reply to her "clever political letter" of 1942 Mann noted that "your thoughts echo mine." Indeed, as the war drew to an end and the Nazi minions toppled in flames, Mann grew ever more international-minded. Invited by Radio Free Berlin to return to Germany in August 1945, he refused. He had felt that even the United States had a long way to go in the social struggle. "I was so glad to hear from you again and share your political anxieties with full understanding," he had written to Mrs. Lowe on February 18, 1945.

One is almost sorry for this fair country. Its people had anticipated that after the war was over one could start again where one had left off. But now the nation becomes aware that this is not possible, that it is being carried along in a world revolution—of which the war is only a part, the least weighty one in fact. Life will have to be lived differently, and naturally there is fear of that. The fear of peace is great everywhere, and I believe the majority of men wish that the war would go on for a long time, because they see it as a kind of shelter, protecting them from the grave problems that will confront the nation and demand to be faced. An inkling of what is to come is in everybody's mind by this time, with the outstanding awareness that nothing can be resolved from a purely nationalistic standpoint. Two factors cannot be evaded: one of these is world cooperation, the other tending towards Socialism, i.e., a systematized economy. The human problem is how it will be possible to combine economic planning and discipline with the widest political and cultural freedom. In Europe, Russia will have the greatest influence because it alone has found a real and honest solution for the calamity of unemployment. It does not, however, seem to wish to impress its methods upon others. For America, the conservative socialism of a Roosevelt and a Wallace, which wants to preserve a capitalistic society, surely is the right form. . . . We have here a socialistic democracy, which this country better than any other nation can well afford. I am still confident that it will prevail, though it sometimes seems as if the refractory blockheads will make it dangerously difficult. Surely these fellows would not recoil in fear from Fascism and all its aberrations if they could put a stop to social progress. And yet I believe the sane common sense of the people as a whole will be stronger than they are, and I *have still to unlearn my faith in the good will that is the dominating force in American life.* [Italics added.]

This last sentence serves as a key to Mann's *volte-face* about Germany and the Germans. Once the die was cast, he became an ardent American, believing (or hoping) that the United States held the open-sesame to a New World— both politically and socially. He held a deep faith in the working classes, which, he believed, under the leadership of Roosevelt and Wallace, would become a model for socialistic democracy. Unfortunately, Mann was politically naïve, and at the time of the victory over the Nazis had no knowledge of the reactionary forces only biding their time until the war, which had silenced them momentarily, was over. His naïveté encompassed the Soviet Union, which, he believed, "does not seem to wish to impress its methods upon others." The facts of *Machtpolitik,* of course, contradicted him, as Russia absorbed East Germany, Poland, Czechoslovakia, Romania, and Bulgaria, and stretched its bear's paw in the Orient toward China, Korea, India, and Japan.

Mann had been trying to arouse Germany to the danger of being absorbed in the Fascist mélange since just after World War I; his warnings, as we have seen, fell on deaf ears. He continued to push Germany toward the democratic, socialistic side even after the war—notably in *Doctor Faustus,* in which he described the Germans as pathological specimens who must resort to medical treatment to recover from the grandiose dreams of world conquest. His appeal fell on barren ground—witness the storm in Germany over *Doctor Faustus.* "My heartfelt thanks for your letter," he wrote to Mrs. Lowe on February 15, 1946.

I fully understand your warning or rather dissuasion which is contained in your praise of the indirect effect of a work of art. However, I decided long ago that I shall say nothing further to the Germans. Whatever I have said has only served to arouse them, in spite of the fact that the emigrants were always enthusiastic. Perhaps that was already a bad omen. The difficulties of an understanding between those who are inside and those who are out is considerable. In this matter, therefore, there will be nothing from "my lips," as Platen says in one of his poems. I doubt, moreover, whether the Germans will be grateful to me for *Faustus* before the expiration of from fifty to seventy-five years.

In 1949 Mann visited Germany for the first time since 1933—to receive a "Goethe Prize" in Frankfurt-am-Main. He enraged many West Germans and their new anti-Soviet allies, the Americans and the English, by proceeding to the Eastern Zone to accept another Goethe award in Weimar. Miss Ida Herz, another German refugee from Hitler, was deeply disturbed by Mann's visit to East Germany and complained to Mrs. Lowe. "I disagree with you about T.M.'s Weimar visit," Mrs. Lowe replied on August 28, 1949. "It was brave of him, and sure to be misunderstood but in face of the ridiculous anti-Soviet government campaign in the USA and England, it was, or will be sometimes viewed as—salutary." ("This was an answer to my fears that T.M. would again be drawn into the internal quarrels of 'ever-divided and never-united Germany,' " Miss Herz wrote to me. "I had lived with him through all these violent attacks before and after the Nazis came to power, and I had seen and felt how his health and his peace of mind—which were so necessary for his work—had suffered.") The publication of *Doctor Faustus* in 1948 stirred lively debate both in the United States and in Germany. Mann was correct in doubting that the Germans would be grateful for *Doctor Faustus*, which was regarded as libel in many places. "The often extremely vile attacks against me by the German press sometimes get on my nerves," he wrote to Miss Herz on December 1, 1949. "What a distasteful people these Germans are—of course with some estimable exceptions. But never will they determine Germany's physiognomy." He was looking for co-operation from international-minded men of good will from all the nations—and Germany did contain some of them.

Mrs. Lowe was in full agreement with Mann by this time. "Our point of disagreement," she wrote to Miss Herz, "is about Germany. And of course here T.M. would disagree with you too, for your position, basically, is that there are no 'good Germans.' I agree that they are in a shocking and repulsive mess; but the fault or crime is not wholly of German making, though you all love to dramatize yourselves and think that it is!" She resorted to doggerel to express her feelings about the rather smug attitude of an America flushed with victory:

THE TASK

Come, let us teach the German youth
And lead it in the way of truth.

122

In Another Language

Let's send our teachers trooping o'er
Directly we have won the war
And stamp the German evil out
And send it to the rightabout.

Oh, Bismarck is a herring
And Wagner is a law,
And Heinie was a Dutchman
In our other glorious war.
And Goethe was a vandal,
Or wasn't he—oh, pshaw!

For we know how the thing is done,
Under the flag that makes us one:
We cram our youth with history's lore
As never youth was crammed before,
And while we pile it on so thick
We wonder why it doesn't stick.

Oh, John Brown was a body,
And Hamilton a fish
And Uncle Tom a pancake
That was Lincoln's favorite dish.
And Lexington's a derby hat
You bet on if you wish.

Come, then, and let us show the Hun
Just how these little things are done;
And how our institutions free
Instruct us all in history.
And when we've taught him to forgo
The ancient lies he used to know,
Let's fill his mind with facts like these
And murmur "Just forget them, please"!

Oh, Hamburg is a beefsteak
And Frankfurt is a dog,
Berlin's our only Irving,
But they're all in such a fog
We are bound to go and tell them—
And just won't we make them slog!

Libra

The postwar years from 1946 to 1954 were indeed trying to men of good will in all countries, but particularly in Germany and the United States. German "war criminals" were being tried and executed in Nuremberg; the inevitable "America First" reaction had set in just as the United Nations was assembling at Lake Success. The Soviet Union was exercising its veto power at the United Nations and extending its frontiers in Europe and the Far East. Some bitter American nationalists were demanding withdrawal from all foreign affairs save business; others demanded that the United States drop the atom bomb on Russia as a preventive gesture. The Manns were shocked and frightened at the hysterical atmosphere they encountered both in Germany and in the United States. "California is now a veritable paradise," Frau Mann wrote to Mrs. Lowe on June 18, 1946; "however, it is impossible to take joy in this environment in view of the disturbing and frightening conditions that prevail in the world." Thomas Mann, nervous and excitable as he was about world problems, threw himself into the international arena by signing petitions, joining committees, and writing articles. He had reached the conclusion that the true future of the world could be attained only by an international socialistic workingmen's federation.

Mrs. Lowe, who had taken quiet satisfaction in the way in which Mann had come around to her position, was formulating her political and social notions in a long series of letters to her nephew Charles Lowe. These letters she considered to be of special, even of paramount, importance in a world which seemed to her already heading for another great war precipitated by economic and political rivalries. Mann agreed with her "remarkable letters to your nephew," adding: "There is much quiet thought and reason in your words which is a great blessing today. I for one must admit that the poisoned, hysterically tense and disaster-laden atmosphere in this country depresses me and is not exactly profitable to the state of my nerves and my energy."

Mrs. Lowe felt that the United States and England were heading for a dangerous split—a split between the working classes and the power elite of finance capital. Because huge profits depend upon a wartime economy, this power elite was driving these two countries into another holocaust, which, with the hydrogen bomb, might well end civilization as we know it. When Winston Churchill delivered an address at the Massachusetts Institute of Technology in Cambridge, she wrote to Dr. Charles Lowe:

Winston Churchill is a very great man. He enjoys the deep veneration and heartfelt gratitude of the western world. He made a noble and stirring address to the scholars, scientists and public men gathered at M.I.T. Much that he said was only too true.

But suppose he had stood up and said:

"Another war is not to the interest of any of us. As for my own country, it cannot possibly profit anyone. It would probably not survive one. The same is even more true of the nations of continental Europe. As for this country, rich, victorious, resourceful and free, it could not profit either. It would face single-handed a chaos a hundred times worse than the present one. It could not, by itself, preserve our civilization. And in that mortal struggle the very liberties we should be fighting to preserve would themselves be jeopardized. Who then would profit? Many individuals would make much money, achieve much power. Science and knowledge would make further giant strides, whether constructively or destructively for us, we cannot know.

"All governments are and must be actuated by the best interests of their own people. War is today to the interest of none. I believe we ought to keep these facts clearly in mind."

No, Winston Churchill could say nothing like this. He would be as unpopular as Jesus the Christ.

"In simple words I mean that a split can be avoided if people will discuss their differences," she wrote at this time to Alfred Knopf. "This split I mean is national, and if the people on both sides refuse or are scared to talk, the nation will certainly lose the strength of unity. Perhaps it has lost it already."

Mann agreed with her substantially, particularly on the problem posed by the hyper-nationalists: "The political conditions in this country do affect my nerves, as they do yours," he wrote on February 18, 1950. "I do not even want to look into the daily papers. The most alarming are those *New Leader* socialists who insist on the manufacture of the 'hell bomb' and who call [Whittaker] Chambers an admirable martyr. It is horrible! That there still exist nonconforming forces which continue to encourage you to speak, fight and protest is at the same time both a comfort and a torment."

That Mann, whose political and social acumen Mrs. Lowe had grown to respect as much as she respected his art, sympathized with her attempts to slow the nationalistic drive to war, heartened her. In 1951 she outlined the background of her stand in a letter to him:

My education in a radical position began very long ago, to be exact in 1902, at the time of the so-called Reading coal strike. I took to reading then, and by slow stages, what with books and speeches and events, became in a general way and not very emotionally (or very thoroughly, I fear) an adherent to a Marxian interpretation of our society, and later an assenter (I do not know how to put it more colorlessly) to the revolution as described by Shaw, the Webbs, and the Fabians. . . . If I may make so pompous-sounding a statement, I do today adhere on the economic side and on pragmatic grounds to a socialist position. And on the political side to no very enthusiastic adherence to any government, since it is clear to me that each must act to the interests of its nation, and what governments today mostly find to their interest is pretty generally an anachronism.

Not all their letters were on political matters. Toward the end of 1949, when Mrs. Lowe was "finishing off and polishing up some of my own unfinished trifles," Mann sounded her out on the translation of *Der Erwählte*, an easy, short novel to give relief from the ponderous *Doctor Faustus*. On December 18, 1949, Mrs. Lowe replied:

I should of course be delighted to see some of your ms— though as usual with misgivings, and perhaps with more misgiving than usual, because, as last time, I shall need extra assistance in addition to the usual fee. . . . I need not tell you how important it is to me to have some intelligent person working with me, not only for the actual typing and comparing, but also for the stimulus and encouragement of the companionship of even a paid person. I had such a person in England and owe to her some of the success, such as it was, of the English *Faustus.*

Mann went to Knopf with her suggestions and wrote her on February 18, 1950: "Alfred and I came to an agreement very quickly concerning assistance for your work. Encouraged by this circumstance, I am sending you more ms., quite a pile, pp. 145–253." He then made an unexpected comment upon his own work: "My inclination towards the comic must be curbed for the sake of the religious seriousness of the subject, which is, after all, the background."

He was writing about what appeared in English as *The Holy Sinner,* his modern treatment of the medieval German legend by Hartmann von Aue of the incestuous origins of Pope Gregory the Great. It was only after considerable soul-searching that it became *The Holy Sinner.* Mann did not like the literal English for *Der Erwählte,* "The Chosen One," as he wrote on December 10, 1950:

Let's drop it. There is quite a choice of English titles for the novel. In the beginning I thought of something like "The Story of the Great Pope Gregorius." But I am afraid that with that too much is anticipated. Next came "Sin and Grace" to my mind. It is not impossible, nor is "The Holy Sinner." What about "The Sinner Who Was Chosen"? But that may rather be a subtitle. One could add the names of the two and say: "Gregory, The Story of a Sinner"—"Made of Sin" would perhaps not be bad either. Nor would "Son of Sin," still better with the addition of the name, "Gregory, Son of Sin."

You should propose all these titles to Alfred together with one or two of your own invention. He knows best what is attractive.

Of one thing he was sure, that "on the title page only the more familiar form 'Gregory' should appear. Americans don't know how to pronounce 'Gregorius' and would be frightened."

In a less condescending mood, he added: "You have a lot of opportunity to *dichten*. There are many more or less hidden verses and rhymes in the story. 'Sibyllas Gebet,' for instance, is composed after the mode of an old prayer to the Virgin."

Mann had written this letter in answer to one from Mrs. Lowe, writing from her home town, Towanda, Pennsylvania, on December 1, 1950, in which she described her approach to the problems of a medieval tale:

I have read it—and have even begun to translate it, for— did I ever tell you that I can never even see the problems until I get it away from the German? I am delighted with its simple charm; of course there are problems; but if there are none in the rest *of any different character* from those I already see, I think I can manage. It would help me and expedite the work if you could tell me the things you read: of course the Gesta Romanorum, then there are the Roman de la Rose, and the Chanson de Roland, the Arthurian Cycle, Froissart, Malory, oh, endless other things—but I have to acquire a vocabulary and a rhythm and there are of course medieval English versions of all these, if I knew how you went about it. It is great fun!

It was fortunate that she thought it great fun, because in certain ways, particularly linguistic, it was the most difficult task of translation she had ever done for Mann. She had to acquire a knowledge of Old High and Middle High German, of Old French and Flemish dialect. One can feel her medieval sources in the quaint English that emerges. She even checked at the New York Planetarium the eclipse supposedly seen on the Island and assured Mann that it could not have been seen on the Island at that time. The resultant translation pleased her and Mann exceedingly. Mann wrote her in English on October 25, 1951:

In New York . . . Knopf gave me a copy of *The Holy Sinner,* and I have since occupied myself a great deal with your translation. I have good reason to write to you and to express to you my gratitude for your achievement and your patience and, as far as I can see, the highly successful elimination of all difficulties which also in this case, and perhaps particularly in this case, presented themselves. Better judges than myself have acknowledged your success, as I saw from many reviews. One might even say that on the whole you got off better than I did, for, with the exception of the warm article in *The Atlantic Monthly,* the literary comments written by the leading papers were more or less lukewarm and without any real enthusiasm or understanding for the book. I have long since been used to this and mind it even less as the reception by the public has been especially friendly.

It was well that the translation pleased them, for it was to be the last work Mrs. Lowe was to do for her dear "Tommy." *The Black Swan* (*Die Betrogene*) she did not like, and the translation was given to Willard R. Trask; when she was offered *Felix Krull,* she first said no and then yes, but by that time the book had been given to Denver Lindley.

She had not, however, given up translating, for she did one more book [3] for Lion Feuchtwanger, to whom she

[3] *This Is the Hour,* a novel about Goya, translated with her daughter, Mrs. James Fawcett (The Viking Press, New York, 1951).

wrote one of the shrewdest comments on the problem of translating for the English and the American reader: "Any translator for both markets must encounter this difficulty," she wrote from London on May 26, 1953—"a sort of international impasse—and struggle against the emasculation of style which is prone to be the result. And if you avoid Scylla you may fall into Charybdis, i.e., you commit what Mr. Shaw called 'translator's little treacheries': what you have done is a portrait, not a photograph, of the original."

She also translated several poems for Hermann Broch, who wrote: "To have a poem translated by Helen Porter-Lowe is, of course, a high honor and joy, all the more so as in my opinion the poem is much better in English than in German."

When refusing *The Black Swan* in May 1953, Mrs. Lowe explained: "The reason is perhaps silly: in the end of my life I have so many things in my head that I find I must get them down, whether they ever find a publisher or no." One of these "things" had come from her head to the typewriter and was going the rounds of the publishers in England and the United States—fruitlessly—unhappily for Mrs. Lowe, who did want some printed evidence of her own creativity. *Sea Change,* her tentative title, is a tale of a sexual metamorphosis of twins—Francis, the sensitive adolescent boy, and Flora, the tough-minded, strong-bodied girl, children of an American couple on vacation in Brittany. It is based, in part, on the French fairy tale of Friquet and Friquette, but the physical background reflects the happy vacations that Dr. and Mrs. Lowe had spent in Brittany. Its ironic and sometimes shockingly comic overtones are clearly in the Mann tradition; but the substance and language are unmistakably those of Mrs. Lowe. The best criticism yet written of *Sea Change* was rendered by Thomas and Katia Mann in a letter written from Zürich on August 11, 1953:

We would both like to thank you for the pleasure you have given us with your work. On the one hand, it is understandable that publishers may draw back hesitatingly from this uncommon kind of offer and have little faith that a wide public will be sympathetic to this strange novel-poem [Mann was still smarting from the cold reception that *The Black Swan* had received—sales running far under the optimistic estimates of Alfred Knopf]. Still, both of us regret this hesitation, which, after all, need not be the final word. For, quite aside from the poetic treatment of nature, the intimate relation with the sea, and the lively descriptions of people and places in Normandy which this novel contains, the theme of the book is not only original but is treated with stylistic skill and a special kind of psychological intensity. You can well imagine that the subject matter of the work, especially the psychological treatment of the body-versus-soul relationship, struck a familiar chord which made me feel at home, you might say. The two attractive main figures, Francis and Flora —the sensitive, sophisticated boy and the coarser, happy-go-lucky girl—are entirely convincing in their mutual dislike until their fantastic episode of a purely physical switch of their sexes; in fact this American professor's family spending its sabbatical in a small French seaside resort comes vividly and realistically to life. Even after the miracle the plot holds the reader's interest and becomes actually dramatic toward the end, when Francis the girl barely escapes drowning, while Flora the boy eagerly participates in the rescue of the formerly hated one. This opens comforting vistas into the future of the two children so strangely transposed by a freak of nature. You, who are re-creating and reviving the story of Friquet and

Friquette, are basing your plot on the conciliatory wisdom of the fairy tale: anyone able to live within another, be it even for only one hour, would change from an aloof to a knowing and sympathetic person. It must be admitted, though, that doubts arise when one sees the mother starting on the return trip to the United States with the twins, and one begins to wonder how, for heaven's sake, the two creatures can and should live henceforth. I think it is possible that this aspect of the story might be the one to offend and run into trouble with the publishers. As for me, this objection, even if it might be justified, does not change my interest in your book, and my wife shares my feelings. Both of us wish to thank you for giving us the opportunity to become acquainted with this original strange production and we both hope that you shall have the satisfaction of seeing it published.[4]

In thanking the Manns for their keen insights into *Sea Change*, Mrs. Lowe wrote from London:

I am deeply grateful for your letter. You and Frau Doctor have understood it in a way I hardly dared to hope. I too think an appeal to Alfred would be useless. Though I personally felt

---

[4] In the confusion attendant upon the move from one house in Switzerland to another, the Manns had lost the manuscript of Mrs. Lowe's novel, *Sea Change*, and Mann wrote abjectly on May 19, 1953: "We often think of how you may be getting on and ask ourselves how you may be feeling toward us in your heart of hearts concerning the ugly trick that was played on you by us or by the complications of circumstances. There is, of course, much confusion when the contents of a crammed-full house, inhabited for a long time, are transported into another house, and this in the absence of the owners. They have been leading a wandering life for many months, going from hotel to hotel, until they found relative quiet in this little house. You would not believe what I myself have lost in the way of manuscripts, books, gramophone records, but all these losses touch me less than the loss you have incurred, of which my conscience continues to remind me. Where the first part of your manuscript may be remains an obscure enigma. We continue to mull it over and do not give up hope that it will be found somewhere and somehow. How gladly I would then read the whole of your work and plead its cause with Knopf with a determined letter."

133

that what with the present popularity of the ocean in print and the fact that the little story is about the tragedy of parents and their children, it might produce a slow and modest sale instead of a total loss. The points you raise about the difficulties of life in America after the metamorphosis I have also thought of and think I could do something about it if the matter ever is raised. . . .

At present I am writing a lecture story and a long satire in the manner of Pope, but have not much hope for either of these things.

"I just had a letter from T.M., who *is* working *langsam* on *Felix Krull*," Mrs. Lowe wrote to Ida Herz on November 28, 1951. "What you write about his interest in the beginnings of life rather stuns me, because it is so much what is (in my novel) preoccupying me. Maybe we ought both to be occupied with its other end. But I do not believe it."

During most of her life Helen Lowe was a good practicing agnostic, but she had received a pious Protestant upbringing in Sunday school and church, and toward the end of her own life she began to rethink the beginnings and end of life itself. "I hope you'll try to adopt, slowly, my attitude of faith towards life," she wrote to Miss Herz earlier in the letter just quoted. "I am not, truly, a religious person, but quite literally I have checked up on the events of my life in reference to a line of a hymn I learned as a child: 'Better hath He (never mind who) been for years than thy fears.' Probably you do not feel like that, and probably you have reason. But I have mainly on this ground almost stopped fearing. One reason is that we don't (psychologically speaking) realize what it is we are actually fearing."

134

In Another Language

She was fearing, like almost everyone else, the atom bomb and its threat to the continued existence of mankind. To exorcise this fear, she turned to satiric poetry:

PERADVENTURE

O mighty atom, baby bomb
Upon our Circle burst like this,
We greet you, Per,[5] while part in fear
And part in joy that you are come,
We ask if fear be more than bliss.

No doubts we feel about our bliss;
Our hearts rejoice that you are come;
And yet a fear—forgive us, Per—
Intrudes on an event like this
Advent of an atomic bomb.

We shudder, thinking what may come
To our poor world beset like this.
Comfort us, Per, pray calm our fear
By proving a benignant bomb
And turn our terrors into bliss.

Who knows, with engine such as this
More mighty still than any bomb,
You'll free, dear Per, our world from fear,
You'll prove the organ of our bliss
And all creation's joy become.

In 1957, when she was in the middle of a distressing period of melancholia, she turned, again in poetry, to a power above herself:

[5] Per was her godson.

135

O Lord, if Thou art yonder more than here;
If Thou art then, not now—or sooner every-when;
If Thou has made us in thine image, not we thee in ours;
If let a single sparrow fall to earth, Thou Demiurge
 dost see and mark
It may be thou in modest turn wilt mitigate
Our sheepishness, our shames and our despairs.
For faith we pray with hearts a-weep.

Mann had written his letter about *Sea Change* from Erlenbach, Zürich, whither the Manns had moved after selling the house they had built in California. Toward the end of her article "On Translating Thomas Mann," Mrs. Lowe states:

I am somewhat hesitant to comment on the circumstances which caused Dr. Mann and his wife to leave the U.S.A. and take up residence in Switzerland. . . . A recorded broadcast on the BBC two years ago [1951] is a forthright statement in which he says that he, no Communist, refuses to "take the anti-Communist shilling.". . . A series of episodes has, I should guess, made American residence distasteful to him, as it has to a fair number of Europeans who once sought and found in it a refuge from persecution. Such people are mostly private individuals; their discomfort is no less keen for being largely subjective. I think it reminds them of their flight from Europe in the dread decade of the thirties. Now there is nowhere else to go.

Why did the Manns leave their adopted country? This brings us back to World War II, when England, Russia, and America were firm allies, united in their struggle to destroy Fascism and Nazism forever. When Mann became a convert to democracy and an American citizen, he condemned dictatorship, whether Fascist or Communist, as the essays in *Order of the Day* prove. When the Soviet Union was attacked by Hitler in 1941, Mann, like Churchill and Roosevelt, welcomed Russia as an ally. In 1943 he was given his first opportunity to attest to his friendship for this enemy of Nazi Germany. "The occasion to send letters of greetings to Russia, offered by the New York branch of the Russian War Relief to us in America, comes unexpectedly," he wrote to Mrs. Lowe, "and I gratefully avail myself of it." For years professional patriotic groups like the American Legion had been keeping lists of all who indicated the faintest sympathy with the Soviet Union, branding the sympathizers as Communists. Many good Americans—President Roosevelt himself—were called Communists or fellow travelers, tarred with "guilt by association" by these super-patriots. Later, even President Eisenhower was accused of being privy to the Communist conspiracy to dominate the world. As the Cold War succeeded the Allied victory, the tempo of the semi-Fascist patriots speeded up. The Whittaker Chambers–Alger Hiss case, which brought Richard Nixon into the limelight, sharpened the issues. The Korean War, which set the American forces in the United Nations army against the North Koreans, who were furtively supported by Red China and the Soviet Union, almost precipitated another world war. Good Americans began to scream "Communist!" or "Fascist!" at other good Americans. At this point Senator McCarthy headed the senatorial committee for investigation of alleged subversive activities, which branded as un-American every public figure who would not bow down and shout: "To hell with Russia!" These were times to try men's souls and spirits.

No wonder that Mann could write from Zürich on July 7, 1950: "We are supposed to be back in California the end of August. I am a little afraid of the hysterical atmosphere of America. This country is very quiet and sensible." He did return to California, and in January 1951 the press announced that he had joined the American Peace Crusade, generally accepted as a Communist front organization. Early in February, Mrs. Lowe wrote to him:

I am writing two letters to you: one about Gregory [*The Holy Sinner*] and the other about the political situation as it touches you. I saw in the press that you have joined the "American Peace Crusade," and I admire the courage of your act (if, of course, you are not misrepresented), though, coupled with Paul Robeson's name, any "peace" move is bound to be printed in quotes and to brand you as a "Communist"—save the mark! Yet perhaps it is thus that you have decided to resolve the dilemma which faces every "non-Communist radical" (these are days of double entendre, so I must put the two words in quotes too, however literally and earnestly I mean them). I too face this dilemma like other Americans, and though I am certainly an unimportant figure, whose declaration of allegiance to either side could scarcely cause a ripple, I am going to put my position down in writing.

On February 9, Mann answered her letter in a depressed mood:

I enclose the Letter to the Editor, which I sent to the *Times* as soon as I caught sight of the story. It tells you what the course of events was. The letter could have appeared on the 7th. But it did not appear even yesterday, and it seems almost as if the paper would suppress it without even notifying me. . . .

I am deeply depressed and disgusted by all this and if you were to ask what my hopes are I should have to say that I have none. All the forces who wish to avert disaster are without influence and are blundering; the masses are apathetic, fatalistic and consistently ignorant; the workers are without political know-how, and destiny obdurately takes its course ruled by ignominious laws. No book, no matter how good, nor one word of truth which may still be uttered will serve to stop it. I fear that this country will come to learn dreadful lessons.

Your letter, with its friendly thoughtfulness and circumspection, is a model pattern.

In his rather longish letter to *The New York Times*, Mann had objected to his link with Communism under the headline ROBESON, MANN JOIN NEW PEACE CRUSADE, explaining that Paul Robeson's agitation "against his country and mine" was "utterly alien to me, however heavily America's present foreign policy may weigh on my mind." Furthermore, he explained, "a respected American submitted to me a plan . . . aimed at the mobilization of the American people's desire for peace." He then listed seven persons who "could not possibly be suspected of being Communists." Fortunately, Alfred Knopf, somewhat less naïve politically than Thomas Mann, prevented the publication of the letter because, as Mann explained on February 27, 1951, to Mrs. Lowe, "he found the names of the initiating sponsors to whom I referred were all 'very bad,' no better than Robeson. I have sent a short communication to the United Press to this effect: considering the increasing difficulty of recognizing the origin and background of peace movements and popular resolutions, I have determined not to take part in any political or culturally disguised mass appeal. I shall say what I have to say, exclusively on my own account. I consider the United States foreign policy disastrous and sponsor peace but do not wish to do this together with people who might justly be suspected of doing this not for the sake of humanity but for the sake of Moscow."

Later in March, the magazine *Freeman* charged that "Thomas Mann has consistently formed connections with Communist-front organizations." The article made no charge that Mann was a Communist, but said that "he kept company with Moscow-inspired operations." Interviewed by a reporter for the New York *World-Telegram*, Mann vigorously denied the charges and voiced his decision "not to sponsor any more causes, movements, crusades and the like, whether they concern things political or present themselves in a cultural guise."

Apparently he kept his word about signing nothing political or cultural, but he had been given rough treatment in the press and longed for the comfortable anonymity of Zürich. "Your lines gave me great pleasure," he wrote in English to Mrs. Lowe on March 26, 1952.

We are just about as fair as you. We cannot complain. However, as regards the shockingness of the great world, there are many things to complain about. But I can only repeat your question: What can one do? I used to risk quite a lip, but I am tired of having malicious ignoramuses drag me through the political mud, and so I keep my mouth shut—with a pretty good conscience, for I frankly admit that I have largely lost interest in this country whose citizen I became under Roosevelt. We would like to sell our house and go to Europe "for some time," not to Germany, of course, but to Switzerland, which is neutral territory, after all. But the settling of our affairs here is not so simple.

Back in Europe, his true homeland, though still a citizen of the United States, Mann settled in Zürich. The removal to his "beloved Switzerland" was not an altogether happy experience for Mann. On April 4, 1953, he wrote to say that he was sending Mrs. Lowe the manuscript of his new novel, *Die Betrogene* (*The Black Swan*), asking for her opinion of the work:

It has practically been wrung from a very poor state of health. The adaptation to a Central European climate was much harder for my physique than I had expected. The autumn was most unpleasant, the winter a very hard one. The question whether we did right to leave our fine house in Pacific Palisades occupies me continuously. Finally I fell seriously ill —with a virus infection from which I am recovering very slowly. All during this time I was distressed and ashamed about having lost or mislaid the one volume of your novel manuscript. You have every reason to be angry with me. But all this is connected with the new upheaval in our existence, which strongly resembles that of 1933 and equals a second emigration. Much confusion and disturbance connected with it affected my labile temperament. But perhaps we have done the right thing, after all.

Mrs. Lowe, as we have seen, did not translate *Die Betrogene*.

In Zürich, Mann turned to one of his favorites, *Felix Krull*, which he determined to bring to a conclusion. In 1923 he had published *Bekenntnisse des Hochstaplers Felix Krull: Buch der Kindheit*, a fragment of a novel, which Mrs. Lowe had translated for *Stories of Three Decades* as "Felix Krull." In the Preface to *Stories of Three Decades* (1936), Mann stated that "I was not surprised to have many excellent judges pronounce it the best and happiest thing I had done. In a sense it may be the most personal; at least it expresses my personal attitude towards the traditional, which is both sympathetic and detached and which conditions my mission as an artist. . . . I was not destined to return to *The Confessions of Felix Krull*," he concluded regretfully. "I am very busy with work on the Krull Memoirs," he wrote Mrs. Lowe on December 18, 1953. "So much new material for them has piled up that I am considering the idea of having a preliminary volume published next fall. After all, that is just what I did with the Joseph stories. It remains an uncanny idea for me that you will no longer be my English interpreter. It seems very dubious to me that an equivalent substitute has been found or will be found. But your health and your work take precedence."

Mann's regretful comment on the ending of his professional connection with Mrs. Lowe was meant deeply and sincerely. That the woman who had translated his favorite "fragment of a novel" should not complete it was a bitter pill to swallow—for both of them. But Mrs. Lowe had begged off on grounds of health and her own work; then, when she decided to accept the book, it was too late. Another translator had been engaged.

On July 21, 1954, Mrs. Lowe wrote to Mann:

I feel sure I acknowledged the receipt of the proof sheets of Felix. I have now read it and I do lament that I can't see how, with every desire, I could successfully translate it. That is due to my own difficulties, not because of any disinclination. I remember long ago I was enthusiastic about your going on with Felix and said that I would promise if you did, to write the English version. I truly don't see how I can in my present condition.

But do you want me to say what I think about it? You know I explained in that little article "Translating" I never have a critical attitude toward a book of yours when I first read it in German. It is a sort of act of God. You may be sure that I have followed the development of Felix's character with the greatest pleasure and amusement. I cannot foresee what you mean to do with it, although I am sure from the inclusion of the palaeontological material that you intend it to be like the *Zauberberg* and the *Faustus*, a sort of report of our scientific progress to date. I have to confess that it does make more of an impression of the unmotivated than similar chapters did in the other two books. I say this tentatively and with misgivings because I cannot tell how you mean to go on with the book. I can't see that there is any break in the earlier, already translated chapters and this fresh material, but I should like to know if they stand just as they were or if you have made any changes in them.

You wrote at one time that you might have this part published as a separate volume and then go on with the story in other volumes. Do you still want to do this?

When Mann heard of Knopf's choice of a new translator, he wrote his last letter to Mrs. Lowe (September 18, 1954):

. . . we cannot change anything in this affair, and I cannot tell you how much I deplore this. You well know how much I regretted at the time your decision to give up all translation work; and it would have been a comforting thought for me to know that the Krull was in your trusted and well-tried hands. We often think of you, from whom we have not heard in a long time.

Cordially,
Thomas Mann

This marked the end of their professional but not of their personal relationship.

In her letter Mrs. Lowe referred to her "difficulties," which were neurological. In her seventy-eighth year, she was failing and knew it, but she refused to give up. "Neuroses never hurt anybody except those whom they paralyze," she wrote to me from London on July 16, 1954. "I would love to see you and tell you all about my recent experience in 'Bedlam,' which is a Health Insurance Hospital for those who are treated psychologically. It would make you laugh and cry at the same time, which was my reaction. I could only stick it for three weeks."

That she was far from being paralyzed by her "difficulties," she shows in the conclusion of this letter:

As for me, I am still pegging on very slowly and discouragedly. I just had a play of mine turned down by the BBC Third Programme, after much encouragement, and my little novel [*Sea Change*] has been for months now in the hands of agents. Meanwhile I am trying to put into shape a series of essays on political and literary subjects. The one I am anguishing over now is called "The Justice of Justice"—on Capital Punishment —and an anthropological treatment about which I really don't know enough to write. Then there is "Critique of Pure Treason" and some nine or ten others. You don't want me to make you my literary executor, do you?

In March 1954, Mann wrote to announce that he had bought a house in Kilchberg am Zürichsee and to complain about a film being made on the biblical Joseph, "with my novel completely ignored. This is really scandalous . . . but I can do nothing to stop this, as the biblical theme is entirely free from copyright; yet it seems like pure nonsense that today a Joseph film should be made without taking note of the book which has refashioned the story anew for our age."

On June 27, Mann reported that he and Katia had finished reading Mrs. Lowe's "On Translating Thomas Mann."

It *was* a happy idea to write this unassuming and yet charming piece of personal autobiography based on your work as a translator. For me this document telling of our long collaboration, whose end I shall ever regret, was most affecting reading. All the problems of translation, in fact re-creation, the measure of devotion and most meticulous empathy which it demands, are cleared up for the general reader who has no conception of them. The contrasting of the literal, more or less impossible translation with the accomplished free transposition, as well as the juxtaposition of the examples of the two translations of the short Goethe poem, is well done. You have said much that is good and pertinent in a concise way, and I would be sincerely glad to see the work appear together with the Faustus essay.

In 1954 Mrs. Lowe returned to the United States, settling in Princeton, where, after several years of illness, death came quietly to her on April 27, 1963. One last link between Mann and his translator rests among her papers:

A BIRTHDAY ODE

June sixth, 1875–1955

Thomas Mann on his 80th birthday
by Helen T. Lowe-Porter

Humility befits the modest muse,
The shorter garment is the kind to use

For one who aped the master's organ tones
Distuned with feeble pipe what was his own,
Transposing his sustained philosophy
Into a flatted and resonant key
That oft has missed a note in bass or treble,
As oft laid down the lute, unstrung, unable,
Indeed the metaphor's unapt, what though!
Of all the arts 'tis music paired must go
With mathematics, she's the most exact:
From science had her birth and joined her pact.
To keen-edged words, to cloudy poesy
We weak resort to celebrate the day
When he was born, the master of the two.
Music and words, precision harmony, who
Garbs in two arts philosophy profound,
Where intermits the copious flow of sound;
But moves from strength to strength, nor can he fail
Whilst marvelling we his majesty must hail.
All hail then, master of the word and tone.
Capacious heart, unerrant ear and brain!
May strength be granted, may thy years be more
Amply increased, to add for us their store
Of high-piled images of massive worth
Whilst we rejoicing celebrate thy birth
And from thy bounty we no less dare ask
Than conscious harvest crowning constant task.

What Mann thought of this tribute we do not know, for
he died of an embolism on August 12, 1955.

But the association of many years' standing was not to
end with Thomas Mann's death. On June 23, 1956, Katia
Mann wrote from Kilchberg am Zürichsee, where her

husband had quietly penned his last lines on a lapboard, looking up from time to time to survey the proud expanse of the Zürichsee.

Dear Mrs. Lowe:

I have been wanting to write you for a long time; let me assure you that I have often thought of you and am thinking of you, of our contact which lasted more than a lifetime, of everything that you did for him and his work in England and the United States. But I have so much to write and it is all so hard for me. Now, the arrival of your article [6] gives me the welcome occasion to be heard from at last, and I thank you heartily for having had it sent to me. We read it together at some time in the past and discussed it—and if I remember rightly you had doubts of publishing it, while he advised you strongly to do so and was pleased with these very personal notes giving a picture of the painstaking artistic work of a translator, so little appreciated. I reread your essay on translation now with the same feelings and remembered our talk about it and it touched me deeply.

There is not much I can say about myself, I need not tell you that my life no longer has any true meaning. Though there is much to be done, almost more than is commensurate with my strength. My two dear grandsons, Toni and Frido, are staying with me, since their parents are always partly in the United States, partly in Europe. Erika is in Kilchberg most of the time and Golo is here at the moment. As you see, I am not alone, however—

Please accept my hearty wishes and greetings,

Yours,
Katia Mann

[6] "On Translating Thomas Mann."

TWO ESSAYS

by H. T. Lowe-Porter

DOCTOR FAUSTUS
(1948)

by H. T. Lowe-Porter

"The road of excess leads to the palace of Wisdom."

WILLIAM BLAKE

O f *The Magic Mountain* Ludwig Lewisohn once said
that it was a novel written with the full intellectual
equipment of the first quarter of the twentieth century
(I have not got his exact words by me but this was their
sense). Lewisohn's was probably the best summary
comment ever made on that great work. A quarter-century
has passed. And now: to write with the full intellectual
equipment of this second quarter of the same century,
this dazed, disequilibrated, disintegrating, yet pregnant
time; to state it, to give it contour and content with the
tools of intellect and art—since I, at least, feel that such
was again the author's function—was that in any way
possible?

It is considered to be the office of great art both to utter
and to interpret its age. It may seem to do this either with
immediacy or over a period of time; the effect is achieved
in both ways. And the statement appears to apply to each
one separately, of what we call, collectively, "the arts." The
question then is: could a single novel—as it were, a *Don*

Quixote of a novel—possibly perform the feat of expressing and interpreting the second quarter of the twentieth century? I submit that the answer is affirmative.

The theme of *Doctor Faustus* is the invocation of the demonic. The framework of its plot follows roughly the legend in the sixteenth-century chap-books: this modern Faust studies theology, shifts to magic (music), makes a pact with the Devil, is shown by him the marvels of the universe and enabled to compose works of great genius. At the appointed term he is not, literally, carried off by the Evil One, but figuratively he is, for he suffers a stroke and for the remaining ten years of his life is wholly mad. One should note that the reader may accept the actuality of the Devil and the pact or not, as he sees fit: the narrator leaves the question open. If not, then he may conclude that the hero was insane throughout—or again, he need not, just as he likes; for there is still a third alternative, to be mentioned later. In passing: Dr. Mann has definitely made the legend more acceptable, since this Faust is a further development from Goethe's and Marlowe's, to name only the two greatest versions. Marlowe's Faust asks to be great emperor of the world, to slay his enemies and to aid his friends, to live in all voluptuousness, etc. Goethe's hero desires not only to quench his fiery passions in the depths of sense; what he wants is a life of productive activity as opposed to thought: *"rastlos bethätigt."* But Adrian Leverkühn sells his soul that he may *create*, in other words *be* God, and that in a field whose rewards we conceive to be higher than all the traditional gratifications of power or sensual enjoyment. Perhaps the highest vouchsafed to man. We can to some extent acquiesce in the bargain—if it was that and not a figment. We do so today the more readily in that our ideas about sin are both more confused and more compliant than they were in the sixteenth or even in the eighteenth century.

Adrian Leverkühn—"Bold Liver," we note the name— lives from 1885 to 1940, though his reason and his creative powers come to an abrupt end in 1930 (we note the date). He was born on a farm not far south of the Harz Mountains and spent his schooldays in a provincial town to which Dr. Mann has given the name of Kaisersaschern. People, Dr. Mann tells us, can vote the Social Democratic ticket at the polls and yet live in a medieval atmosphere of folklore and demony, partly grotesque and partly uncanny. Pockets of such air have survived in ancient towns and in the country; much less in modern urban societies—but still . . .

Adrian never quite shakes off his provincial origins. As a musician of genius he is cosmopolitan-minded, drawing nourishment from the cultures of the world. As an individual he is unsocial, self-conscious, uneasy in society, devoid of warmth in human relations. Even his music betrays the influence of his background. His nature is "cold." Its only apparent relaxation is in a crude sense of the ridiculous which cannot fitly be called humor since it is in essence humorless. For Dr. Mann's purposes Adrian had to be sceptical and superstitious; passionate and frigid; an artist and a scholar; provincial and cosmopolitan. As all these things together, he could stand for "Faustian man."

Save for two chapters, the twenty-fifth and the forty-seventh, a dialogue and a monologue, he seldom speaks for himself, save in the music he creates. The narrative is

153

put in the mouth of a professor of humanities, his close and adoring friend since childhood. There are at least two reasons, perhaps three, why there is this confrontation of humanism and science. In the first place, though less importantly, it is decisive for the style. The professor may speak, as professors do, in good literary and academic accents; so that the tale is told at a leisurely pace, and while occupied with matters of the most burning immediacy for our day, is stylistically a nineteenth-century novel, very possibly the last—or the last but one. In the second place, the two characters, hero and hero-worshipper, are a deliberate, at times almost forced confrontation of the humanistic and the anti-human. As complementary figures they recall—of course with differences—other such contrasts in Dr. Mann's novels: Tonio Kröger and Hans Hansen; Hans Castorp and Joachim Ziemssen; Naphta, Settembrini and Pieter Peeperkorn, etc. Indeed, Dr. Mann and—Dr. Mann. And all of them with variations present the conflict between the lawless and the disciplined within the personality of the artist. Structurally the *Faustus* exhibits a further development and elaboration in Dr. Mann's technique of giving symbolic relationship to everything—plot, settings, characterizations. In short, it is as though the author's aim in his own art were to achieve the "strict style" which is the ideal of his hero's music: a thematic engagement and involvement, with the intention to leave no "free note." The *Faustus* exhibits the same preoccupation with time that was a striking feature of *The Magic Mountain*. It is timidly advanced here that the involutions of the time-dimension employed as a technique by modern novelists (the earliest instances I know are in the work of Joseph Conrad) may represent approximations of our shifting point of view with respect to the element of time.

Leverkühn's powerful and brilliant intellect has all too easily surmounted an exacting and exhaustive musical training, mastering not alone every field of technique but the whole history of the development and significance of his chosen art, and a comprehensive general culture besides. Thus equipped, he discovers no little distaste and misgiving, no little suspicion of the tricks of the trade involved in composition. He says: "The work of art? It is a fraud. It is something the burgher wishes there were." One supposes him to have been reassured by his teacher's retort that art needs just such sceptical, bored, fastidious natures, that she may shake off the banal, the epigonal, the no longer functional, and free herself for fresh advance. Adrian has meanwhile been studying at the Protestant University of Halle, where he has, to put it like that, added survival value to his childhood memories by reading theology and listening to an exposition of medieval theories of sorcery and the black arts. He now removes to Leipzig, where he takes a doctorate in philosophy and at the same time begins composing.

What should such a one compose? As baldly summarized thus far, his situation sounds almost too contrived a temperamental conflict, almost too obviously the Faustian pattern. It is lent psychological inevitability by the narrator's shuddering-adoring analysis—in other words, of course, by Thomas Mann's unfailing power of evoking human reality almost as a visual experience, though he explicitly says, in Chapter XLIV, that this is an impossible feat. Adrian is unique, a genius; but at the same time he and his art can only represent his age of disintegrating norms and ironic gropings. (One difference between him and Tonio Kröger is that he is by no means so articulate.)

He outgrows his earliest productions even while he sets them down. In flight from the banal, he chooses parody as the only musical expression possible today and writes a mocking, technically brilliant and highly unpopular opera. The adjective applied to it was "decimating" (perhaps crushing?). It was condemned as a speculation in notes, more academic than artistic. Leverkühn is defending the thesis that music is an art by nature ancillary; he next composes settings to a considerable volume of poetry, English, German, French, and Italian.

The composer's personal and his musical development move along parallel paths: his cold aloofness from human kind and the willful strangeness of his music spring from the same root. (It seems Mallarmé had already said that *"toute maitrise jette le froid."*) Here we shall follow his history in more literal and less symbolic terms than would be furnished by an account of his creative development— though one questions indeed whether the outwardly uneventful course of the man's life gives much hold for a detailed accounting. One sees at once that he was not born for marriage and family ties. He early left the parental home without apparent reluctance and, as was said of Goethe, he never visited his mother again. After the catastrophe she came to him. Another allusion, this time to Nietzsche, is present in the pregnant incident of Leverkühn's one outburst of sexuality, with its fatal physical issue, so dwelt upon and linked with genius in the sinister dialogue with the Protean Evil One. This dialogue follows the canon, and also there are reminders of the "gentleman in the sofa-corner." In our day Bernanos has written *Sous le soleil de Satan* and Paul Valéry an elegant ballet-like encounter of Faust and Mephisto (one is flippantly reminded of that ancient anecdote in which a Frenchman and a German each write a monograph on the elephant). James Hogg's early nineteenth-century *Confessions of an Acknowledged Sinner,* with its protean Satan, has lately been republished in England. And I am told there is a new German novel wherein he figures in person (I have been unable to get the title). Who knows how often the tale has been told? Often enough to serve as evidence—if any were needed—that man is perennially occupied with the problem of evil. The dialogue between the Devil and Adrian takes place in Italy and vividly evokes that atmosphere of adoration of the classic Mediterranean world so characteristic of the lettered German and so apposite to his northern mysticism.

The composer returns to Germany and takes up residence on a Bavarian farm, the local traits of which are weirdly like those of his own birthplace. A man of no ties or few, and those initiated by others; in somewhat delicate health, dependent upon a degree of simple comfort and care; like Chopin, "not wanting to know"; confined to all appearance to the splendid complexity of his aural images, an ear- not an eye-man, and withal not perfectly convinced that heard melodies are sweeter than ditties of no tone. After his single abortive sexual experience, he leads, according to the professor, on the human plane a chaste life, monotonous in events and contacts. But in the book as a whole there is large variety of character and incident, each one, or almost each one, contributing to the organic design: artists and scholars, friends and sycophants, the

impayable impresario, the "human" landlady, the recalci-
trant famulus. Some of these are vivid personal reminis-
cence, inimitable, convincing (a few not so much so, in
the way nature sometimes has of being less natural than
art). A young violinist represents a rare and late experiment by Adrian in the sheerly human: a charming, gifted,
flirtatious adolescent, he pays with his life for having
wooed and won the composer. For now, at forty-four
Adrian decides to marry, and the woman of his choice, a
young professional designer, rejects him in favor of the
violinist, who then is shot by the young man's jealous
mistress. Similarly, the adored lad, upon whom the author
has expended his utmost in loving evocation, falls victim
to spinal meningitis and dies after prolonged agonies
described in piteous detail.

These involvements of the plot, however, fit quite tightly
into the main design. One hesitates but one decides that
their inner significance belongs not only to the interpretation of the plot but to the plot itself as well and must
therefore be included in this bald accounting. I mean that
the pact with the Devil bans human love; thus the diabolic
exigency of the composer compels him deliberately to
sacrifice the violinist, with whom he had begun an "unna-
tural" love affair in the delusion that such will be counte-
nanced by the Evil One. He does this in a sufficiently
involved and unpleasing way, by tricking the young man
into an engagement with the identical young female
whom he himself ostensibly designs to woo, thus deliver-
ing over the youth to the vengeance of his discarded
mistress. Again the expressive landlady is likewise undoubtedly "thematic." She may parallel, in a minor role,
the character of Pieter Peeperkorn in *The Magic Moun-*

tain. And the adored little lad dies a victim of his uncle's evil eye—had not Adrian, long before, as theology student at Halle, learned that "the tender substance of little children is especially susceptible to the poison of such an eye"? All this is of unexampled gruesomeness. Finally the migraine, the niggling nausea, and prolonged spells of vomiting to which the composer is periodically subject are gone into exhaustively because they form part of the penalty exacted in exchange for supernatural creative élan. As always, the clinical picture is surveyed with horrifying relish.

In the final scene of the hero's "rational" life, following the pattern of the Faust book, he is made to summon his friends (*magistros, baccalaureos, et alios studiosos* [masters, bachelors, and other students], actually the musical and intellectual world of Munich) and to reveal to them in a sort of "elder" language all the circumstances of the pact, the demonic and filthy sources of his art, the murders he has done, his concubinage with a succubus in the form of Hans Andersen's little sea-maid, and other supernatural soliciting. He sees no loophole from his fate nor any hope of pardon save, pitifully, that he has toiled and moiled, and "who seeks hard things to him it is hard." (We think of *"rastlos bethätigt."*) Essaying to play from the score of the *Lamentations,* he falls in a seizure. This scene and the concluding Epilogue, in their reserve and realism, are of crushing effectiveness. One feels a bottomless dejection.

Such is the routine of the plot, which I have set down as though the work were a novel like another. But it is not like another, for it has such implications as suggested the question: can any single work of art command the full intellectual equipment of our day? Could it weave for us the garment we see our time by? *Doctor Faustus* deals with a German genius, with the German nation and with an art which, though like all great art, universal, is yet in a sense a peculiarly German art. I feel there is a risk that many readers may take the novel as applicable merely to the German nation and people. I am concerned that the universality of the critique be pointed out; that we should be aware the bell tolls for us too.

The protagonist of the story, Adrian Leverkühn, writes the kind of music that we call "very modern," and we are given to understand that the extended critique of it and of music in general throughout the work applies to music first, but to all the other arts no less. In one of his rare expansive moods the composer says: "Isn't it amusing that this art for a long time considered herself a means of release, whereas she herself like all the arts needs to be redeemed from a pompous isolation which was the fault of the culture-emancipation, the elevation of culture as substitute for religion—from being alone with an elite of culture, called the public, which soon will no longer be, which even now no longer is, so that soon art will be entirely alone, alone to die, unless she were to find her way to the folk?" Again: "The antithesis of bourgeois culture is not barbarism but collectivism." And: ". . . the whole temper of art will change, and withal into the blither and more modest—an art *per Du* with humanity."

Thus the artist. But it is the foul fiend—or is it only the artist's diseased fancy?—who makes the most devastating synthesis. In the dialogue (Chapter XXV) he says: [1]

---

[1] Mrs. Lowe's quotations are not identical with the published version of her translation of *Doctor Faustus*. She probably altered them here in the direction of a more free-flowing narrative within her essay. [J.C.T.]

"What is art today? Look at them, your colleagues, your fellow-inaugurators of the new music, I mean the honest, serious ones, who see the consequences of the situation I speak of . . . not the folklorists and neo-classic astylists whose modernness consists in forbidding themselves a musical outbreak and in wearing with more or less dignity the style-garment of a pre-individualistic period. . . . They are powerless too; but I think we prefer the decent impotence of those who scorn to cloak the general sickness under color of a dignified mummery. Yet the sickness is general, and the straightforward ones show the symptoms just as well as the producers of back-formations. Does not production threaten to come to an end? And whatever serious stuff gets onto paper betrays effort and disgust. . . . Composing itself has got too hard—devilishly hard. Where work does not any longer go with sincerity, how is one to work? But so it stands, my friend: the masterpiece, the self-sufficient form belongs to traditional art, emancipated art rejects it. . . . It comes down to this: that his (the artist's) compositions are nothing more . . . than solutions of technical problems. Art becomes critique. That is something quite honorable, who denies it? . . . But the danger of being uncreative—what do you think? Is it perhaps still only a danger, or is it already a fixed and settled fact?"

In his valedictory address Adrian said: "I felt all too well that it is the time when uprightly and in pious sober wise naught of work is to be wrought and art grown unpossible without the Devil's help and fires of hell under the cauldron." So with the Devil's help he wrought strange things. Of his early work the narrator says: "It contains, on a developed musical plane, against a background of extreme tensions, banalities, of course not in a sentimental or complacent sense, but rather in the sense of a technical primitivism . . . specimens of sham naïveté, audacities dressed in the garment of the primitive. . . . They often affect one like at once a mockery and a glorification of the fundamental, a painfully reminiscent ironic treatment of tonality, of the tempered system, of traditional music itself." At this time Adrian expounded to his friend his idea of the strict style, derived from the way in which melody and harmony are determined by the permutations of a fundamental five-note motif. He explained the "magic square" of a style of technique which yet developed the extreme of variety out of identical material, and in which there is no longer anything unthematic. This technique, he said, admitted no note which did not fulfill its thematic function in the whole structure—there was no longer any free note. Furthermore, the professor felt that Adrian's work tended more and more to the hybrid. He repeatedly expressed the view that the old distinctions between chamber music and orchestral music are not tenable and that since the emancipation of color they merge into one another. As for the symphony in one movement, cynically entitled *Marvels of the Universe*, Zeitblom brusquely calls it "out-and-out mockery, bizarre and unpleasant." Of the settings to some of the poems of William Blake he says: "The composer has set these darkly shocking verses to simple harmonies, which in relation to the tone-language of the whole had a 'false,' more heart-rent, uncanny effect than the most daring harmonic tensions and made one actually experience the common chord grown monstrous." Of the amazing score of the puppet plays based on the *Gesta Romanorum:* ". . . the

harmonically most dominating, the rhythmically laby-
rinthine, was applied to the simplest material, and again a
sort of children's trumpet style to the most extraordinary."

While meeting with much opposition and dislike, the
composer's reputation had slowly grown, though he himself was far from giving encouragement to those who were
interested in what he wrote. Some portions of his works
were performed during the twenties—the names of living
conductors are mentioned. His oratorio *The Revelation of
St. John the Divine* (*Apocalypsis cum figuris*) was given
in Frankfurt in 1926, the professor says; he describes it as
a synthesis of the whole ecstatic literature of pre-Christian
and early Christian eschatologies, holding up to humanity
the mirror of the Revelation, that it might see what was
oncoming and near at hand. It, and the last work, the
cantata called *The Lamentation of Doctor Faustus,* were
the composer's two most important productions. Of each
there is a long description in the words of the narrator,
from which I excerpt a few passages of horror-stricken
comment: ". . . the awful scream given to the mocking,
bleating bassoon, the wail of the Bird, or the harsh choral
fugue on the words of Jeremiah: this a reference back to
the archaic fugal forms of certain canzoni and ricercari of
the pre-Bach time . . ." "roaring brass passages, heavily
scored and widely spaced out, which make one think of an
open abyss . . . the quasi-ecclesiastical music of his later
years." Again: "The enormous difficulties which every
rehearsal and performance present have directly to do
with the late and cultural revival of the cult in art . . .
which seizes upon means that belong to a stage of civilization not only priestly but primitive." And: ". . . sounds

that begin as mere noise, like tom-toms and thundering gongs, savage, fanatical, ritual, and end by arriving at the purest music . . . this gehennan gaudium . . . what acoustic panic results from the repeated drum-glissandos," etc. "Or take as another example of easy technical facility in horror, the effect of being at home in it . . . the loud-speaker effect . . . the incidental jazz, used to express the purely infernal element—one will bear with me if I apply the word *streamlined* to a work . . . whose basic mood has more to do with Kaisersaschern than with modern slickness." The professor wistfully tries to confute some of the charges (e.g., that of cultural bolshevism) made against it, protesting that it contains certain lyrical passages which are like a fervid prayer for a soul. Of Leverkühn's last and loftiest work (the symphonic cantata *The Lamentation of Doctor Faustus*), the narrator says: "In my zeal and love I am bound to call it matchless. . . . *The Lamentation* . . . is expression itself; one may state boldly that all expressivism is really lament: Nature's melancholy Alas! in view of man, her effort to utter his solitary state." "Echo, favorite device of the baroque, is here employed with unspeakably mournful effect. . . . It does not lack significance that the Faust cantata is stylistically so strongly and unmistakably linked with the seventeenth century and Monteverdi . . . only that here the dialectic process appears as endlessly more complicated in its logic than in the time of the madrigalists." "A Utopia in form of terrifying ingenuity, it becomes universal . . . causes the whole work to be completely swallowed up by thematic thinking. . . . A mammoth variation piece of lamenta-tion—as such negatively related to the finale of the Ninth Symphony." "The music thus lifted beyond the structural

element or within its utmost severity . . . can yield itself
to subjectivity." "It sounds like the lamentation of God over
the lost state of His World." "The uttermost accents of
mourning are reached. . . . [There is] no other consolation than what lies in giving sorrow words; in the fact that
a voice is given the creature for its woe."

For lack of space I must forbear to quote further,
though what has been quoted so far may not be enough to
avoid a false effect of abruptness and baldness. Yet I hope
it may be enough to lead up to the statement that Dr.
Mann draws an explicit parallel between his hero's demoniacally inspired music and the anti-democratic, anti-humanistic philosophy which was taking shape in Europe
and which resulted, in Germany, in the Nazi regime.
Professor Zeitblom refers to certain advanced views discussed among Munich "highbrows" in the time of the
Republic. These ideas gravely disturbed his humanistic
soul, the more in that he saw them mirrored in the art of
his friend Adrian. These discussion evenings set about our
professor shrewdly; the more, because at the same time he
was sharing intimately in the birth of a work which had
certain bold and prophetic associations with these same
conversations. The professor quaintly says that his worry
made him lose twelve pounds' weight.

Dr. Mann takes as useful peg a work by Georges Sorel,
Réflexions sur la violence, published in 1907. "The group
who practised critique," says the humanistic professor,
"were men of education, culture, science. They did it,
indeed, smiling; with a blitheness and intellectual compla-
cency which lent the thing a special, pungent, disquieting,
or even slightly perverse charm. It is probably superfluous
to state that not for a moment did they recognize the form

of government which they got as a result of defeat, the freedom that fell in their laps, in a word the democratic republic, as anything to be taken seriously. . . . With one accord they treated it as ephemeral, as meaningless from the start, yes, as a bad joke, to be dismissed with a shrug. . . . Even more trenchant and telling were the perception and statement of the fact that in this age of the masses parliamentary discussion must prove entirely inadequate for the shaping of political decisions; that instead the masses would have in the future to be provided with mythical fictions, devised like primitive battlecries to release and activate political energies. This was in fact the crass and inflaming prophecy of Sorel's book: that popular myths, or rather those proper for the masses, would become the vehicle of political action: fables, insane visions, chimeras, which needed to have nothing to do with truth or reason in order to be creative. There was no doubt that in the future, after we had begun to practise a large-scale elimination of the unfit, the diseased and weak-minded, we would justify the policy by . . . hygienic arguments for the purification of society and the race. Whereas in reality the real reasons lay far deeper down, in the renunciation of all the humane softness of the bourgeois epoch, in an instinctive self-preparation of humanity for harsh and sinister times which mocked our humane ideals; for an age of over-all wars and revolutions which would probably take us far back behind the Christian civilization of the Middle Ages; in a return to the dark era before it arose after the collapse of the classic culture. . . . The Munich group amused itself by imagining a legal process in which one of these mass myths was up for discussion in the service of the political drive for the undermining of the bourgeois social order. . . . The fantastic thing was the mighty apparatus of scientific witness quite futilely invoked to prove that humbug was humbug. For the dynamic, the historically creative fiction, the so-called lie, was simply inaccessible to this line of attack. Science, truth—good God! The group could scarcely contain its mirth at the desperate campaign waged by reason and criticism against wholly invulnerable belief. What they envisaged, indeed, was like the most novel setting-back of humanity into medievally theocratic conditions and situations, and that was as little reactionary as though one were to describe by the word the track round a sphere. . . . There it was: progress and reaction, the old and the new, the past and the future, they became one, the political Right more and more coincided with the Left." In these pages too, the self-stultifying nature of the freedom-principle is all too convincingly set forth.

Sorel's book was published forth-seven years ago, and, be it noted, was written by a Frenchman. It was very widely read. The time, it seems, was waiting for it. And of course there were others. They are well summed up in the sententious remark of the Evil One in Chapter XXV: "Reality? Is not reality what works?" Here we have the philosophy of Nazism, pragmatism gone mad.

The passages quoted from the work and more like them indicate Professor Zeitblom's human and political attitude. Surely in many a characteristic turn he speaks for Dr. Mann, as a device for making clear to the world at large the point of view of a cultured anti-Nazi German. With more personal reference the professor remarks: "I have never, precisely in the Jewish question, been able to agree fully with our Führer and his paladins: and this fact was not without influence on my resignation from the teaching staff here. . . . Today my two sons serve their Führer. . . . I have only to imagine that through some unlucky chance they became acquainted with the contents of these pages and in Spartan denial of every gentler feeling denounced me to the secret police, to be able to measure the abysmal nature of this conflict." About the bombing of German cities Zeitblom says: "I share with no small part of our population, even those hardest hit, the feeling that we are only getting what we gave." And he greets the annihilation of his nation with mingled horror and rejoicing, also with that overwhelming sense of sin which the Western world has never ceased to require from the people of Germany. At the very end of the book he conceives of her too as partaking of the Faustian symbolism and being carried down by demons to the bottomless pit.

So Adrian, so his land, so his art. There is no hope, no redress, no escape from the horrid hents of hell described by the Devil himself in that amazing bravura passage in Chapter XXV. One had not supposed that a material hell could have anything for us any more save cold boredom; but here some drops of authentic horror are expressed from it. Perhaps such receptivity too is a sign of the times; perhaps we too are undergoing a "merciful narcosis," a ripening to an awareness of the airs which Adrian breathed in his childhood and moved in when he studied theology at the Protestant University of Halle. Perhaps, as Professor Zeitblom says, our time itself tends to return to those earlier epochs: "it enthusiastically re-enacts symbolic deeds . . . that strike our modern age like a blow in the face." (But he was, of course, speaking of Germany and Germans.)

Leverkühn, reared in the Lutheran faith, and Zeitblom, a practising Catholic, attended in Halle a course of lectures on the psychology of religion given by a sort of Mephisto-Goebbels. They were of a very advanced intellectual kind; for the lecturer's demonic conception of God and the universe was illuminated by psychology and thus made acceptable, yes, even attractive to modern scientific thought. Adrian probably scoffed inwardly at them, but they found a stratum of acceptance in his subconscious mind. We should scoff too, of course. These lectures, in themselves a brilliant tour de force, a feat of suggestiveness, give opportunity for comment on the state of matters religious then as contrasted with the way things were in the Age of Faith. For instance: "Precisely because medieval man had received a closed intellectual frame from the Church as something absolute and taken for granted, he had been far more imaginative than the burgher of the individualist ages; he had been able to surrender himself far more freely and sure-footedly to his personal fantasy." On the other hand: "One sees clearly the infiltration of theological thinking by irrational currents of philosophy, in whose realm indeed the non-theoretic, the vital, the will or instinct, in short the demonic, have long since become the chief theme of theory. At the same time one observes a revival of the study of Catholic medieval theology, a turning to neo-Thomism and neo-scholasticism. On these lines, theology, grown sickly with liberalism, can take on deeper and stronger, yet more glowing hues; it can once more do justice to the ancient aesthetic conceptions which are involuntarily associated with its name. But the civilized human spirit, whether one call it bourgeois or merely leave it at civilized, cannot get rid of a feeling of the uncanny. For theology, confronted with that spirit of the philosophy of life which is called irrationalism, is in danger by its very nature of becoming demonology." Elsewhere the professor quotes Schleppfuss, the Mephisto-Goebbels, who in one of his lectures, describing a case of witch-burning, says as follows: "God in His loving-kindness made the woman fall into the hands of the Inquisition. . . . Willingly did she go to her death, with the express declaration that she preferred the stake in order to escape from the power of the demon. . . . For she had fallen away from God, and that was superstition: easy belief in the instigations of the enemy of the human race." We note that it was not easy belief in the Devil but easy yielding to his infamous solicitations which constituted the sin. One sees that these comments are, in the field of theology, a pendant to the political and sociological conversations among Munich savants which distressed the liberal and humanistic soul of our Catholic professor. Zeitblom is no less revolted by Adrian's anti-humanism when the composer recounts to his friend the marvels of science, maliciously describing the horrendous modern discoveries of astrophysics as displayed to him in person by the Evil One in the guise of an American professor. The Faust book is here followed with grisly effect to present a sort of summary of the latest news about the marvels of the heavens above and the waters under the earth. We are reminded of a like scientific chapter in *The Magic Mountain*—also of the Temptation in the Wilderness, to which I would not refer if similar parallels were not drawn in Chapter XLVI of the novel.

Here, now, at this point, it is in place to return and confront the theme of *Doctor Faustus* (which I have sought by such copious quotation to make clear) with typical themes of discussion and writing we everywhere meet today. I gave as a summary characterization of the theme of this novel "the invocation of the demonic"; in other words the appeal to powers other than human and rational, other than those which we explain by the processes of our reason; such powers as our humanistic pedagogue, while not denying their existence or their influence, has always found utterly foreign to his nature. It would be ponderous and disproportionate, even if I were competent, to insert here a compendious accounting of current European and American critique in the fields of art, politics, and religion. I believe also that it would be superfluous. And of course I could not venture to discuss the vast question whether the despair of an age is in fact prone to synchronize with the despair of its art. However, no one, it seems to me, could read *Doctor Faustus* without realizing that in it the "hot" problems of our time of troubles are very definitely being raised. These *are* the things we talk about, the things we feel. The novel crushingly responds to our sense that our world today is at the season of mourning; that we must not seem to scant the present of its dreadful due, but in season fitly and duly mourn, and that art expressive of our state will be the issue of our woe—as in the Gothic time the wry and wailing mouth of the Mother of Sorrows expressed the age's overwhelming sense of sin. What I have tried to do in this article is to be as contemporaneous as possible; to gather from recent books, from the weeklies and monthlies, even from conversations with friends whose words have authority in their various fields, statements to match some of those already quoted from the work. In such passages the epithet frequently used is not "demonic" but inhuman, anti-human, dehumanizing, as in Ortega's book *The Dehumanization of Art.* I quote his title, though the book was published as long ago as 1925, because his condemnation is roundly challenged today by one of the foremost constructivist artists: "In an age when the scientific eye of man is seeing through matter into a fascinating, all-embracing image of space-time as the very essence of our consciousness and of our universe, the old anthropomorphic image inherited by us from our primordial ancestry is still in full sway in the major part of our contemporary imagery. So long as our artists are incapable of seeing in a mountain anything but the image of some crouching naked figure and as long as our sculptors sweat to carve from various angles this graven image, keeping themselves in a state of mind almost identical with that of a Papuan or Hottentot, the sculptor cannot claim to have acquired a new vision of the world outside him or the world in him, and science with all its achievements in advance creation cannot possibly claim to have incorporated its new image of the world into the mentality of mankind." He continues: "Why, may I ask, is not the contemporary artist to be permitted to search for and bring forward an image of the world more in accordance with the achievements of the developed mind, even if it is different from the image presented in the paintings and sculpture of our predecessors?" A Freudian interpretation of much modern, surrealist painting and sculpture does suggest that the artist's unconscious is indeed "inhuman" in spirit. A contemporary poet defines his philosophical attitude as "Inhumanism, a shifting of emphasis from man to not-man; the rejection of human solipsism and recognition of the trans-human magnificence."

Two other arts require covering in this confrontation of current comment and criticism with the same subjects as they are dealt with in the present work. I mean, of course, music and literature, in particular the novel. Not trusting the scope of my own reading, I have asked an eminent musicologist whom I am permitted to call my friend to set down for me what he thinks to be a fair statement of the views held among modern composers on the state of their art today. Alas, it sounds dismayingly like the words of an *advocatus diaboli,* a supporter of the Devil's dictum already quoted from Chapter XXV of the *Faustus:*

"No other score written in this century is remotely comparable with Stravinsky's *Sacre du printemps* in the spell it has cast upon a whole generation of composers. And what is in the score? Hard-driven, inhuman rhythms that crush the individual who attempts to feel with them, rhythms that cut into the consciousness through harmonies that assault the ear with shrill and sombre impact and melodies that are awkward fragments tossed momentarily into the tumult. This music was written in 1912; composers since have been compelled, consciously or unconsciously, to imitate or to avoid the work.

"Some men in later years have written more gently, have prolonged into our time reminiscent methods and an expression precious and nostalgic, out of the 'dark backward and abysm of time.' But those few, those unhappy few whose names are on everyone's lips as the true protagonists of modern man, are frank experimenters, ever more deeply involved in the intricacies of theory and

173

ever more remote from any public save an instructed few.

"It has become incredibly hard to be a composer. A vast technique of many styles must first be achieved. The labor is such that it is small wonder men take delight in displaying this technique and calling it art; but harder still is the search for direct sincerity of expression valid for our time, for a time in which man is less than the machine and contemplation is brutalized by vulgarity."

The reference to Stravinsky recalls to one's mind that his music has been coupled with the prose of James Joyce. Between words and notes there is a vast difference—Dr. Mann has bemoaned in this very book the saving irresponsibility of music as compared with the explicitness of the word. Yet I think we must agree, reading Joyce, reading even Sartre, that in their works words are being used largely for ends other than that of narration as such.

In the field of sociology a Russian philosopher has lately said: "The dehumanization of man has been without precedent. The machine has not only mass-produced commodities, it has converted living men into masses." And he refers to the spiritual phenomenon of the annihilation of spirituality. In a recent magazine article another philosopher has roundly stated that "belief in the ultimate irrationality of everything is the quintessence of what is called the modern mind." Another thinker observes that "under certain circumstances nothing contains more irrational drive than a fully self-contained intellectualistic world-view." A few years ago an English philosophical writer, in one of his more important works, gave it as his view that Christianity continues its existence only because we have no other means of escaping the pitfall of superstition which constantly threatens the human mind. Professor Zeitblom, indeed, feels that we have not escaped the pitfall. There have already been quoted above some words of his from Chapter XI of the *Faustus*, about the University of Halle, where he takes occasion to comment upon the historic conflict between religion and science, faith and reason. It seems unnecessary to dwell here on the pertinence of his comment to much that is published today, especially in French Catholic thought; distraught France being altogether the most fruitful culture in creative analysis of this kind.

Demonology, the demonic; irrationalism; anti-humanism, dehumanization. To "pick up words as pigeons peas," these are the ones we hear and see bandied today, with assent or with dissent. They express a distrust of humanity and human reason.

It is never possible to see back to the beginning of a new thing until long after it has come to its end; we do not know where, during the Age of Reason (which has turned out to be an age of faith-in-reason), distrust began. Fresh avenues opening have now made us suspect that we do not think all our thoughts nor feel all our feelings. But we do not know the values or proportions of the effect upon us of such a suspicion, save that one would say it appears to have broadened down to sit heavily upon many of the farthest-on groups of humanity, visiting them with profound insecurity. And we are equally attracted and repelled: Stefan Zweig speaks of our fear-and-love of the unknown. Going back, here, to the speculation raised earlier: did the Evil One "really," in person, appear to Adrian in Chapter XXV? Or was he an insane delusion of the composer? The latter, of course, say those who have adjusted their senses and reason to the laws we know. But: "What is 'really'? What is real to you is real." There must be standing ground between the two positions; there must be a small spot where schoolmen might discuss whether a thing may be at the same time true and not true: a point at which open-minded, even-handed scepticism is in place. To give one small illustration: in defiance of ridicule, sober work is being done on "telekinetic phenomena"; though an interpretation of the term is given as "operation of a non-physical force which can produce a direct physical effect upon objects." And that sounds uncommonly like "the classic age of faith" as interpreted by the Mephisto-Goebbels lecture in Chapter XIII. But here everything depends on verbal distinctions.

We have learned from the narrator that the Faust cantata was largely composed at the time of the death of little Nepomuk, as a deliberate denial of the Hymn to Joy. And yet . . . The narrator's final comment on *The Lamentation* runs as follows: "For listen to the end, listen with me. One group of instruments after another retires, and what remains, as the work fades on the air, is the high G of a cello, the last word, the last fainting sound, slowly dying in a pianissimo-fermata. Then nothing more; silence, and night. But that tone, which vibrates in the silence, which is no longer there, to which only the spirit hearkens and which was the voice of mourning, is so no more. It changes its meaning; it abides as a light in the night."

Upon our bottomless dejection as we are visited with the final collapse of the man, his nation, his art, this high G of the cello strikes almost with an effect of anti-climax. It seems to say too much; to qualify the finality of the catastrophe, the hopelessness we have embraced as we read. Or is it that it says too little? That it denies us, in that sweet way we were in to despair, the knowledge of just wherein our consolation lies, in just what consists this "light in the night"? Does it merely mean that no hope could have no fear? Is it more definite than that transcendence of tragedy for which we have a classic word? Had in fact the composer just before his death experienced the catharsis and timidly permitted himself to hope? But we are explicitly told that "this dark tone-poem permits up to the very end no consolation, appeasement, transfiguration." Hope is explicitly denied to Adrian, his nation, his art. And to us? It is no part of Dr. Mann's thesis to enlarge upon such a hope, but only to raise it. Perhaps the figure he made his own, the figure of the revolving sphere, taken from Egyptian mythology, is here comfortingly in place. There hope, the instinctive awareness, is not for men but for man: the hope that humanity as such will through time once again resolve the tragic defeats of religion, politics, and art which are incident to the rationalization (in the older sense) of new knowledge out-topping knowledge; since that today has burst our frame and made us retreat disorderly into an anti-humanistic phase as we labor after some viable synthesis of knowledge and faith.

ON TRANSLATING
THOMAS MANN

by H. T. Lowe-Porter

Buddenbrooks, Thomas Mann's second novel, had appeared in Germany in 1901. Some years later the firm of William Heinemann asked me to try my hand at an English version. I believe some other person had already translated several pages of it. I had never read the novel or even heard of it.

The editor with whom I dealt in the matter was Herman Bang. I had done some work for Heinemann before that, having been introduced to him by James Loeb (of Loeb Classics). In 1912 I had translated for the publishing house a book called *L'Ame des anglais,* based in part on Edmund Gosse's *Father and Son.* It was written by a Mme Bulteau, a writer for *Figaro,* and I seem to recall it won a Femina–Vie Heureuse prize. Anyhow it is a charming *jeu d'esprit,* full of perception about the English character. It did not deserve to fall flat, as it did. It was a pity it was published in the war years. The English version had the benefit of Mr. Gosse's criticism. It was done in Oxford, between the births of my two eldest daughters. I enjoyed doing it. Up till that time, the only translations I had ever done were some of Hauptmann's and Sudermann's plays, I feel sure very badly, for the magazine *Poet Lore*, edited by my aunt Charlotte Porter, who thus was the means of introducing many European authors to American readers. Later I had done one translation or a large part of it from the Italian, a book about mountain climbing and exploration in the Karakorams by my friend Dr. Filippo de Filippi.

Well. When I read *Buddenbrooks*, I deduced its author as an elderly man with—I don't know why—a white beard. The aloof disillusionment of mood in the book seemed to me something quite different from youthful cynicism or revolt. Its inhuman detachment persuaded me that the author had arrived at it after a long life and much wordly experience. When I learned my mistake, I learned at the same time something else: that T.M. had been in his youth an editor of *Simplicissimus*. I would not suggest that he derived his sardonic, his "scurrile" (in the German sense) humor from that publication; it is certainly native to himself, one ingredient in his complex nature. I venture to suggest that it is a product of his mixed stock. (His mother was a Brazilian, his father a North German merchant, an aristocrat, and Senator of the Lübeck Senate.) I do not know how much Dr. Mann influenced the temper of *Simplicissimus*. I had spent some fifteen months in Munich (and Bad Tölz) in 1906–7, my first visit to Germany. German had remained largely a foreign language to me. I was enormously impressed by the culture of all the people with whom I came into contact, and knew that my own surroundings had never compared with this picture of solid and sustained intellectual effort.

To me personally *Buddenbrooks* was a welcome and delightful phenomenon; for German novelists and most German dramatists have always been for my taste too sentimental. I certainly preferred the *brutale* to the romantic. I endorsed this backwash of the romantic movement and welcomed "emotion cooled off and served up on ice" (Tonio Kröger).

I translated *Buddenbrooks* in the intervals of rocking the cradle (not quite single-handed, for I had a little maid at £40 a year) and being assistant and professional encourager to my husband's early work. I had understood that the English version of *Buddenbrooks* was to be published by Doubleday, Page; but when it appeared it turned out to be one of the early Borzoi Books, in two volumes, published by Alfred A. Knopf, a firm I had barely heard of. I had lived in Europe so long, I was unfamiliar with publishing in the United States. I do not know much about it in either country now. How conditions have changed! True, I had spent the years 1915–19 in the United States, but these were war years and for me unproductive, save for a little girl born near Fort Ticonderoga in 1917, and caring for my invalid eldest daughter. I did much reading and wrote a few articles, stories, some verse, and one-act plays, the mss. of which have since got lost. I had never tried to get them published.

I greatly enjoyed translating *Buddenbrooks*. Such work can give one a large measure of the pleasures of creative authorship. I got $750 for the two volumes.

Buddenbrooks in English was published in 1924. In 1923 T.M. and Mrs. Mann came to Oxford, and appeared unexpectedly at "Angle House" at the far end of Woodstock Road, almost on Port Meadow, in the village of

Wolvercote. We had bought this house in 1919 on our return to England. No one was at home and the Manns waited, and I feel sure T. Mann looked over all the books in our scanty library (mostly paleographical) and did his best to size up this unknown instrument which—due to the ugly vicissitudes of those war and postwar years— must willy-nilly (and of course unless he could find a better one) serve him to change the garment of his art into one which might clothe her for the marketplace until times changed. That art, with the years, grew ever more majestic and needed more and more voluminous garments. But the dreadful blow was that the true garment, woven by and inseparable from the German original, was hustled out of the booths. How painful this was to T. Mann anyone who loves words can readily imagine. It must be an enormous satisfaction to him that for years now he has been able to be marketed in the original. However, I believe that the American editions, thanks greatly to the able publicity of the firm of Knopf, have always been the most profitable.

So far as I can recall, at this first meeting there was no discussion of *Der Zauberberg,* on which T.M. had been engaged for some years. Nor, indeed, of much else. My memories, as I seek to revive them, are of an atmosphere of stiffness; of not enough common ground; of a certain unreality. I felt shy, ignorant, and insecure. Such qualifications as I had for the role of translator to T.M. retreated from my own consciousness and made me painfully aware of my faulty speaking German and the poor impression I must be making. At bottom, of course, I was arrogantly sure that I was nearly always well aware of the author's larger creative purposes. Indeed, for a long time I kept the

promise I made to myself of never sending a translation to
the publisher unless I felt as though I had written the book
myself. There came a time when I broke the promise: in
the play *Fiorenza* and some of the philosophic discussions
in the novels, I did not feel quite at home in the more
cloudy abstractions, also in some of the many long and
very "German" essays on Richard Wagner. This of course
was due to my own lacks. However, it would be far more
interesting to set down, rather than my own impressions,
T.M.'s own—and these I do not know, in fact I never do
know them, except through his books; there my percep-
tions are keen.

As for his routine, Dr. Mann describes it himself in
"Mario and the Magician." It is, and I believe continues to
be, that stated in a paragraph I have just come across in
The French Theatre Today, a recent book by Harold
Hobson: "The secret of great output, of course, is not
speed, but regularity. It has been calculated that a man
who wrote a couple of pages every day would, if he lived a
fairly long life, produce as much as Voltaire." But there is
of course more to it than that. Perhaps the process is like
the one described by "a certain Herr Brettschneider,"
writing of Goethe's method. T. Mann quotes this paragraph in his essay "Goethe as Representative of the
Bourgeois Age": "There is in Goethe . . . a poetic genius
which is effective when after carrying a thing around for
some time and playing with it and gathering all the matter
that can serve his purpose, he sits down at his table. . . .
When he thinks of something everything he comes across
sticks in his mind and feelings, he tries to knead it into the
bit of clay he is working on, thinking about nothing else
but that." But indeed I feel I am daring in speaking of this

matter at all, since Dr. Mann has never spoken of it to me.

While I was translating *Buddenbrooks* there appeared in the New York *Nation* a comment by Ludwig Lewisohn to the effect that one could only look forward with shudders to any translation of so classic a masterpiece. He withdrew his statement when the English version appeared, and wrote me a charming letter—though in his review he only said the translation was "competent." In fact we used later to compliment each other as the only two people who "knew how to translate."

Thus prepared, and by now being somewhat more acquainted with T.M.'s works to date, having read *Königliche Hoheit* and the never translated *Betrachtungen eines Unpolitischen,* as well as the early essays, I felt, along with much awe, considerable curiosity. I have sometimes put it to myself that my bump of reverence, though superficially large, is hollow; I know there is an element of friendly scepticism in all my judgments of men and their works. So then, regarding T.M. as it were with an auspicious and a dropping eye, I saw him, forty-eight years old, a tallish, slenderish man of good figure, possibly slightly hollow-chested (remember, these are only my impressions), thin at the temples, with a sensitive mouth and hands, blue eyes, dark skin and no traits otherwise remarkable save a fine, bold, jutting nose. He wore a dark-blue pinstripe suit, in the correctest possible fashion, and might have been a businessman, like Hans Castorp's Uncle-Cousin James. His manner was rather dry and stiff, though kindly. The atmosphere of this first meeting was, I believe, a bit conditioned by the war. It took place some five years after 1918, but it was Dr. Mann's first visit to

England and a better time would have been later. The years-long loss of contact, the isolation felt so keenly in Germany—T.M. even voiced it on this occasion, I remember—had its counterpart in English reserve and suspicion. We were fairly intimate with members of the German-Language Department in Oxford, and one of these friends chanced to be giving a large evening party. I suggested that the Manns be invited; but after much anxious consultation the idea was given up, as being "uncomfortable" on both hands. Thus T.M. was denied any but the most modest contacts with the University: tea in the "neutral ground of a café" with a number of the German faculty, and a conducted view of the colleges. His wife and he must have felt unpleasantly like lepers. But certainly they had no "sense of guilt" such as was after 1918 felt to be the proper attitude of all worthy Germans. On the other hand, I should say that T.M. does at present taste this guilt, bearing as he does consciously upon his shoulders the duty of representing the German *"Geist."* His great creative activity must (though of course it did not begin that way) result in part in the lightening of his burden, the great appeasement of his collective remorse. It perhaps accounts also for his political essays. These, of course, represent (in particular *"Kultur und Socialismus"*) the long evolution from the point of view of the *Betrachtungen* to that of "An die deutsche Republik" and "Appell an die Vernunft." I have often in the past pressed T.M. to consent to an English version of the weighty volume of the *Betrachtungen* "for the record," perhaps somewhat abridged. But he had borne too much obloquy even from his fellow-Germans to find it possible to go into it all again. His mind, of course, was surely seething with other creative plans. Of course I cannot too strongly stress the fact that these are only my own speculations. We have never discussed the subject. But I have a feeling that what he wrote of Wagner is true of himself: ". . . what he is working on is never merely the task in hand, for everything else is weighing upon him and burdening the productive moment" (from "Sufferings and Greatness of Richard Wagner," reprinted in *Essays of Three Decades*).

Der Zauberberg appeared in 1924. He had worked upon it for ten years—"and look at it!" The equivocal comment was made to me by an English scholar, who himself did not "like" the book. I introduce it here to point out that T.M. did not have at that time a good public in England. He suffers now from conditions quite unconnected with his books.

Cultured and literary England has always brought itself up more upon the French than the German tradition—heaven knows why the antithesis should exist, but it certainly did, perhaps less so in the America of my own youth. Both French and German of course, in the sense of literature, were in those days possessed only by a limited group of Americans. I am not going into this farther than to say that the average literary Englishman has felt a slight contempt for German "heaviness." The Lewes-Eliot-Carlyle-Froude circle and its influence might and should have affected general literary taste more than in fact it did. England had had her own "three-deckers" of course; but in the late nineteenth century, Kipling announced their demise. Their place was taken, as in Thackeray, Trollope, later Galsworthy, by a series in which the characters vaguely reappear. T. Mann's work has accordingly been reviewed less sympathetically than that of French writers, and no school has been formed. I recall that the reviews of *The Magic Mountain* were rather disinterested; the reviewer in the *New Statesman and Nation* apparently did not finish the book, for he stated that Hans Castorp died in battle.

I received a copy of *Der Zauberberg* from the author in 1925. I spent that spring in Paris, read the novel, and began work there—but I do not recall whether I did any translating. I had great misgivings, almost amounting to an infantile fear, that after all I was not capable of understanding the author's creative purposes—a fear which was not lessened by a letter from Mann himself expressing his view that though I had rendered the *Buddenbrooks* into English *"wie geboren,"* it was scarcely likely that any woman could grasp the cultural parable expressed in the symbolic technique of the novel. That letter should have stimulated me, but it did not, although in theory I was a confirmed and express proponent of what in those long-ago days was called "women's rights," and under my aunt's tutelage had read assiduously the defense of women as human beings. No—partly my pride was touched at the idea of forcing myself into a commercial bargain with an unwilling author; but partly I was really scared, though on grounds not that "Woman" but this particular poor specimen was unequal to the task. This may have been, I tortured myself with thinking, what T.M. really meant. I know he considered my field to be sociology rather than literature. I resigned the work with mingled feelings of pride, defeat, and relief. But now the American publishers, Mr. and Mrs. Knopf, took a hand. I had gone to meet my children in Brittany, where we had a cottage at St.-Caste, on the coast. I met Mrs. Knopf in Paris, and agreed to resume the work provided the author would state that he was willing I should do so. This he did, in a kindly letter more compounded of hope than of faith. I surmised the Knopfs probably represented to him that they would be obliged to pay me for two or three months' work. In 1926 I had finished it, and read the proofs in America, whither my husband and I went to spend the summer.

The Magic Mountain appeared in 1927. In England it had a grudging reception, in the U.S.A. an enthusiastic one. (In general, this has been the fate of all T.M. works.) I thought, and still think, it great, and the best critique of it Lewisohn's oft-quoted one. It enjoys a steady sale to this day. Of how many single novels in the world can Lewisohn's statement be made with any justice? *The Magic Mountain* is only one of T.M.'s of which it can be said; I would contend that *Doctor Faustus* is certainly just as much an epitome of an epoch.

After the appearance of *The Magic Mountain*, I again told Mr. Knopf that I was withdrawing from the work of translating T.M., and he agreed that this was probably wise. The next volumes were done by Herman George Scheffauer, a German-American then living in Munich and editing a collection of translations into German of American novels, to which T.M. wrote prefaces. I remember that Ludwig Lewisohn's *Mr. Crump* was one of these. Scheffauer translated "Der Tod in Venedig," "Herr und Hund," and "Tonio Kröger," which appeared in one volume, now out of print. Also, "Der Tod in Venedig" was translated in the U.S.A. by Kenneth Burke. I cannot remember how long this went on; so far as I can recall, these were the only volumes to appear or be translated up till the time when Scheffauer incontinently fell or jumped out of a window. I know nothing whatever of the background of this tragedy. In the end I was asked to resume, and did so, the next volume being *Three Essays*, i.e., "Goethe and Tolstoi," "Frederick the Great and the Grand Coalition," and "An Experience in the Occult." In all of these essays traces can be found of the theme and trains of thought which took final shape in *Der Zauberberg*.

I am a little vague about the activities of the next years. I remember doing Bruno Frank's *Tage des Königs*, a true *jeu d'esprit*. Bruno was introduced to me by T.M., and I later did another book for him, the novel *A Man Called Cervantes*. It was published by Cassell in London. And at about this time, Mrs. Knopf brought back from Germany some volumes by Frank Thiess; including *Tor zum Leben* and *Der Leibhaftige*. I did not in the least want to translate these books; they seemed to me mediocre, though Mrs. Knopf had taken them as the "best-sellers" of the time in Germany. But in some way which I now forget I appeared to Knopf to be committed to them, so I did them—for my sins, and probably a bad job. I cannot enter into the work of other writers unless their themes and techniques and general *Lebensauffassung* appeal to me as what I should have been employing as original work. And here, I dare say (aside from the dribble of money, which came in very handy in our professorial economy, perhaps a $1000 every two years or so), lies the reason why I translated at all. I had begun this curious task of marrying word-cultures rather superficially, but I think the ground was always the same: the pleasure of using words without the fatal and irrevocable responsibility of using ideas. Shameless, but to an extent true. This great artist, of a controlled mental energy and scope so great it was like nothing I had ever imagined before (because however many books you read, they are only books, not their authors, the pudding and not the cook), was using my ideas and so I used him to give myself private satisfactions. What a tool! What—in short —cheek! It is true I could not wield quite all of him, even in fancy—as I have said.

Eventually I translated "Der Tod in Venedig," "Tonio Kröger," and "Herr und Hund" as they appeared in one volume (1925). I translated "Mario und der Zauberer" and "Unordnung und frühes Leid," the versions by American translators having been turned down by Mann's English publisher as too American.

For part of this time the Knopfs had an office in London (I think in Bedford Square) and published both editions, American and English. The head of this London office was a quaint creature who had formerly been a male militant suffragist and put chemicals into pillar-boxes. I think Raymond Postgate also may have had some connection with the English branch. But finally the English rights became the property of Martin Secker, No. 5 John Street. Secker (and his partner, P. Howe) got out editions of all the translations, including some delightful little single volumes of "Mario" and "Unordnung." I used to like going to see them at No. 5 John Street, and I felt sorry when the firm failed, as it did, some years later. I have a pathetic memory of an interview with them, and of the very likable P. Howe weeping into an immense handkerchief. Mr. Secker later opened a small office in Charles II Street. The publishing rights of Martin Secker were acquired by a new firm, under the style of Martin Secker & Warburg, in offices in Essex Street, Strand, whence they have since removed to No. 7 John Street, Bloomsbury, where they are now, buying sheets of T.M.'s works from Knopf. Now, I believe, copyright laws have been revised, and the English firm resets from the ms.

I have never kept any journal of my translating activities, no dates, no accounts, and the only way I have of recovering them is to attach them to family events. For instance, I have quite a vivid memory of revising the Prelude to the first of the Joseph books while sitting up in a German pension in the autumn of 1933, I think in the Diakonissenheim in Freiburg, whither I had gone because my middle daughter had an appendix operation. Bice had many male friends among the medical students of the University. As she convalesced they came in troops to sit round her bed, play the gramophone (not classics, but *Gassenhauer*), and talk politics. They were pro-Nazi, in a disillusioned sort of way, finding Hitler rather absurd, but expecting him to improve the country's prospects and thus give them jobs. I was introduced as "Bice's mother, who thinks the Party set fire to the Reichstag." I admitted the impeachment; they found me preposterous of course. As for the tales of Jewish persecutions in the previous spring, they called them all lies and foreign propaganda. They used to tell Bice: "*Um Gotteswillen*, do stop saying you are half Jewish!" And: "Mrs. Lowe, you know us pretty well, do you really think any Germans are capable of such cruelty?" They were so decent, these chaps, so little on the whole susceptible to the official propaganda! My reply, to the effect that there were, alas, sadists in every country, my own as well, could not reach their minds. On the other hand, they did not like the Jewish persecution or the dissolution of the trade unions, and they roared with cynical laughter over the K.d.F. (*Kraft durch Freude*,

Strength through Joy). Well, all this is a long way from the Prelude to the Joseph series on which I was working most of the time. This is a rarely beautiful prose poem. So is the chapter "Joseph Stands before Potiphar," in *Joseph in Egypt,* the third volume in the series. I am exceedingly enthusiastic about these two chapters; I cannot rejoice in them enough. Here I might take occasion to express my special feeling for the essay on Lessing, delivered as a speech in 1929, Lessing's 200th anniversary, translated for a volume called *Past Masters,* now out of print, but reprinted in *Essays of Three Decades* (1947). This essay very helpfully crystallized my own anthropological gropings.

In 1934 I translated the second volume of the Joseph series, *Young Joseph,* making, I think, an uneven and indifferent job of it; for personal concerns made it difficult for me to keep my mind on my own work. I have shrunk from going over this book since to search out infelicities which are surely there. The English reviews were perfunctory. My name was occasionally mentioned, with a word or so, "damning with faint praise." What interested and pleased me was that my vocabulary was not spotted as American, this being a point always brought out by English reviewers if they get half a chance. I have throughout been forced—since the English version was for both markets—to emasculate the style, in some degree, taking care to write only what would be acceptable literary usage on both sides of the ocean. I came in time to follow the rule that no word or idiom should be used which was not intelligible, even if unfamiliar, to both publics. I noted that John Galsworthy did the same in his novels. I could and did use both definitely English and definitely American words and idioms; but they had to be understandable to both sides and good literature as well. And they must have no local flavor, either English or American. Sometimes the English or American editor or critic would query or alter a word or phrase on the ground that it was not understandable. When that happened in conversation I always accepted the negative but almost never the positive criticism. It seems few people realize that a character in a novel *must speak in character;* they almost never suggested the right word, while spotting the wrong one.

To return to 1936 and work on *Joseph in Egypt.* I had come back from the U.S.A., and in 1935 had been working on a volume by Franz Werfel, I cannot even recall what it was. In 1935–7 I had a flat in London, with my middle daughter, plenty of time, and good conditions.

Joseph in Egypt fascinated me. I find it T.M.'s greatest imaginative feat to that date and think its power and scope have never had justice from the reading public. He so early became a "high-brow" author! The good work of his publishers and publicity agents so early made it imperative that everybody must buy him who wanted to be thought intellectual that he sold very well, though not overwhelmingly. Probably only a small proportion read, of those who bought. Alfred Knopf once said to me, "You see, Tommy does not know that everything is a racket." This cynicism did not prevent Alfred from seeing that T.M. was really great—nor did it me; so we were both exceedingly glad to make our respective contributions to the fame which otherwise he might have had to wait for in America, and in fact has never had in England, though he has there by now a discriminating if not very large public.

The field of Egyptian archaeology, in my view the most

fascinating of all archaeological fields, was not quite but nearly new to me. I read and worked, worked and read—in poor health, on the whole—but the length of the job of research was shortened in the following way: in December of 1936 occurred the abdication of King Edward VIII, after events which cast a strong and dramatic light upon the state of England and the Empire in those prewar years. I found myself—whose almost daily reading for years had been the Chronicle Plays of Shakespeare—mentally assimilating the modern picture to the Elizabethan scene and stage to a point where the preoccupation interfered with the equally fascinating Egyptian scenario. On the other hand, a translator's work is usually clamored for by publisher and author; it is hard for people to understand why such books as T.M.'s cannot be reckoned out at so many pages a day and turned over to be printed. I am glad to say that Mr. Knopf has never adopted the above view.

I found a student of Egyptian archaeology, a pupil of Professor Glanville, then of the University of London, who gave me the necessary background and English terminology. I finished the play (it was produced in Dublin in 1948 and published by Knopf in 1950) and also the *Joseph* in the spring of 1937.

At this time there occurred the famous episode of the Bonn letter. Dr. Mann had been deprived of his honorary doctorate by the University of Bonn and wrote a nobly inspired and eloquent statement in reply. This famous document has been published in so many places and referred to so often that I will make no further comment on it, except for giving my own personal reactions at the time. The letter was to have been read at a dinner meeting of the PEN Club, and the then secretary of it, the late

Hermon Ould, sent it to me for translation. It was, however, decided that it could not be read at the PEN because of its political character; but I believe it appeared in the *Manchester Guardian* and of course was widely circulated as a pamphlet. It was mentioned at the dinner, and the reason given why it could not be read. I recall that I sat next to Robert Neumann, and that we turned to each other and said in surprise: "But today *everything* is political." Either my memory plays me false, or else this rule was not at all times honored at the PEN, for I seem to recall a meeting in the autumn of 1935 when Jules Romain spoke words of praise for Sir Samuel Hoare's work at Geneva. But to return to the Bonn letter. I agreed that it was a noble document, and displayed full knowledge and lofty indignation over conditions in Germany; less, however, of those in England and France, for it referred to the attitude in the government of those countries as "that of the physician toward a fever patient" or some similar phrase. The words struck a chill to my heart, and I wrote to T.M. begging him to come to England and meet some of the writers—I think I gave the names of a few who would be able to enlighten him. In reply I had a kindly but quite complacent letter beginning: *"Ihr sehr pessimistisch gefärbter Brief."* The next time we met (I believe it was in New York on his first visit to the U.S.A.), he greeted me, as he put out his hand, by saying: *"Doch, Sie hatten Recht."* Which was handsome of him. It is not surprising that T.M. had no great knowledge of English politics; rather more so that he did not estimate the French scene with greater perspicuousness. Most French writers, of course, did not either. On both accounts, however, the weakness has to be laid to Mann's earlier indifference to politics in general. A characteristic of the *Kaiserzeit*, as we all know; and not the only time or place where men of intellect and ideals have found it beneath them to concern themselves with politics. The more the time has cried out for brave intellectuals, the more time has exposed the schism in their thinking. But, even so, we have to distinguish. So far as the domestic, the German scene was concerned, the author of *Betrachtungen* (even though he called himself *unpolitisch*), of "An die deutsche Republik" and "Appell an die Vernunft," and other writings can hardly be said to have absented himself from political thought. And his familiar antinomies, *Kultur* and *Civilization*, are as he uses them political terms in the international sense. However, T.M. has long since explicitly repudiated his former attitude, even [expressing himself] to the contrary. [It must] be set down to T.M.'s credit that he has not been deterred from marking his stages and making his profession of them as he reaches them.

This period, 1935–7, with the beginning of the Spanish war, of "non-intervention" and the general "appeasement" policy on the part of the British government, was a restless and remorseful period for English "progressives." I cannot refrain, at the risk of being thought egotistic, from citing a paragraph written at this time to Klaus Mann, who had sent to the *New Statesman and Nation* (who sent it to me) a letter begging the English world for greater aid and understanding of the tragic lot of the German refugees. I answered Klaus's letter by telling him that no, we could not give him back his native hills and forests. What we could give him was fellow-feeling, "for, believe me, we are not more comfortable in our skins than you" as we survey oncoming disasters. For some reason, the *New Statesman* finally decided not to publish this correspondence.

I began translating *Lotte in Weimar* during that last "peace" summer of 1939—in a rented house with a beautiful rose-garden. I remember how soothing it was to prune the roses, gather the petals and make sachets of them. In general this was not a painful period, rather a rich one with profound human significance. Just accepting as background the certainty of horrors to come made all experience more vivid and precious. *Lotte in Weimar* was very difficult, especially the parts which use a stream-of-consciousness technique to portray the character of Goethe. I think them highly successful, for the reason that (a) nobody was ever better self-documented that Goethe and (b) another great representative of literary Germany had the imaginative power to present him as he was and lived and table-talked. But nobody save a last-generation literary German or professors of German literature in other countries could possibly appreciate the achievement. I worked hard on the English version, and had some help from a refugee, a former editor of the *Frankfurter Zeitung*. I doubt if the book was much read, and the translation when it was noticed at all was reviled, not greatly to my surprise. After all, every translator knows that translating is a sort of trick, a device like the sleight-of-hand operator's to attract attention to something in order to distract it from something else. There is a sense in which all art fits into such a definition—witness the double sense in which the word itself can be used. So also word-craft. When we speak of the little art of translating I am content to have the word used in this double sense. On the other hand I please myself, privately, by thinking of it as a "mystery" in an archaic and now very modern literary sense.

As for *Lotte in Weimar:* the original is a period piece, and as such presented the usual difficulties. I hit on the idea of assimilating the style to the Weimar chapters in Thackeray's *Vanity Fair.* Critics found the result preposterous, awkward, stuffy, and so on. I cannot defend literary translation against the charge that it is a perverse pleasure, and that the translator would be better employed as a philologist or a language teacher. Everybody who ever writes verse or tries to turn a poem into another language than the original, knows that the result, in the measure that it is good as literature, is not the same poem. Try to translate Rilke, for instance! This must be so. Take a translation from Goethe: those happy, facile little lines written by him to commemorate the birthday of his friend the Archduke Karl August:

> *Mit allem Schall und Klang*
> *Der Transoxanen*
> *Erkühnt sich unser Sang*
> *Auf Deine Bahnen.*
> *Uns ist für gar nichts bang*
> *In dir lebendig*
> *Dein Leben dauere lang*
> *Dein Reich beständig.*

Skilled, singable little lines! Dr. Mann quoted them on the fly-leaf of *Lotte in Weimar.* It was decided with his approval that they be left in the original. This is always the better plan, especially in a book like *Lotte in Weimar,* which completely misfires unless one knows something of

German culture. A short time after it was published, a letter appeared in the *Saturday Review of Literature* from Miss Caroline Newton, with an English version of the stanzas by no less a poet than W. H. Auden. I answered the letter by sending the version already made by me and not used. Both versions accordingly saw the light in the *Saturday Review of Literature,* and I give them here with the caution that I am, of course, not absurd enough to compare myself with Auden as either poet or scholar. After all, the original itself is only a smooth and practised little "occasional verse" such as a poet laureate writes to celebrate an anniversary of his liege: here is Auden's version:

> *Though conch and tribal gong*
> *Howl in the marches,*
> *Bold be our rebel song,*
> *Thy courts and arches*
> *Stand. We dread no wrong*
> *In thee made able.*
> *O may thy reign be long*
> *Thy kingdom stable.*

and here is mine:

> *Through all the bounce and blare*
> *Of border races*
> *Our song makes bold to fare*
> *Upon thy traces.*
> *We fear not any wrong*
> *In thee residing—*
> *Oh, may thy life be long,*
> *Thy realm abiding.*

It is clear that Auden's version is the work of a poet. It is eight lines of such verse as he might have written had he been a personal friend of, say, F.D.R. But it is not, I feel, in spirit or technique like the simple warm little patriotic Goethe lines. It does not seem eighteenth-century to me. Auden, I think, cannot be a translator, however hard he tries. He kept the first rule of a translator, to make, not a translation, which is "God bless us, a thing of naught," but did not keep the second (which is to keep the words and the spirit). Or am I all wrong?

This is probably the best place to set down a few comments on technical problems. Of course they apply only to translations from German into English, the field in which I have my only extended experience. I will not attempt to discuss the well-known fact that the German language is both more inflected and more explicit than the English, though German style has been subject in the nineteenth century to a slow simplification, as we know. It is the case that in English not only is inflection at a minimum, but also the train of thought is likely merely to suggest where the German follows through, explaining and expounding. The result is that English is easier to read —unless, of course, you are reading aloud. The German constructs more relative and subordinate clauses, with longer sentences, a different order. So the sentences, in order not to produce a clumsy English, must be broken up —with the result that nobody is quite satisfied. English readers of a translation from the German complain that the sentences still need shortening, while the German author wishes they had not been tampered with. Let me interpolate here that English, perhaps I should say American, style tends to shorter and yet shorter sentences and paragraphs. We are in a great hurry today. Are our modern inventions responsible for the loss of leisure in written English? To return: sometimes the actual order not only of the words but of the thoughts, the logical sequence, differs in the two languages. I recall receiving a scolding from a German refugee scholar for transposing the order of two paragraphs, because it seemed to me the transition would thus be less uneasy for an English reader. I will merely mention here cases where one must rely on the context to get the just translation for a "portmanteau" word like the famous German *Geist*. English has no single word for *Geist;* but it has its own portmanteaux, of course, for instance the very word already mentioned—"art," of which a German critic, however good a linguist, may not always be aware.

There is, again, the matter of dialect. I think it can only be faintly suggested, never localized in a different country. This is a distinct loss, of course. One way of dealing with it is by transferring the bad grammar if there is any. I remember having difficulty with the local (Lübeck) tongue in *Buddenbrooks* and feeling dissatisfied with the result. Idioms, as distinct from dialect, do sometimes, happily, have exact correspondences in the two languages. Where they have not, I have often taken the liberty of using *in another place* the same kind of idiom, pun, or verbal play used by the German author. This will have the effect of reproducing the style in general, though I must concede that, as a kind friend put it, the result is a portrait, not a photograph.

Again, it may sometimes happen that the original sentence uses a verb, noun, or adjective where the idea only exists or can only be adequately rendered—in English

—in a different part of speech. An entirely different sentence-structure results—and another instance of what Bernard Shaw called "translators' little treacheries." These must be called the rigidities of the translator's job, whereas there are relaxations as well: I mean chances actually to translate etymologically—the idea, in other words. A striking illustration of what I mean is Dr. Mann's *The Holy Sinner,* the setting of the tale being the coast of Flanders, the time anywhere between the seventh and eleventh centuries, giving an unexampled and delightful opportunity for linguistic fluidity.

I have sought, lastly, to illustrate some of the difficulties I have pointed out, by giving here a paragraph chosen at random from *Joseph in Egypt,* Vol. II, page 457, "In the Toils." The two versions are supposed to be, first, a literal translation, and second, the same paragraph "tidied up," as it were, into what one fondly hopes is literary English.

IN THE TOILS

"How insignificant, compared with the depth of time of the universe, is the vista through the past of our own life! And yet our eye, fixed on the individual and intimate, loses itself as dreamily, floating in his own early and distant life, as the eye grandly directed upon the life of humanity, moved by the perception of a unity which repeats itself therein. As little as man himself can we dive down to the beginning of our days, to our birth, or further still; it all lies in the first dawn of consciousness and memory, in the small view as in the large. But immediately, at the beginning of our mental activity, when we enter cultural life, as mankind once did, shaping and giving our tender contribution, we come upon a sympathy and a preference, so that to our serene surprise we feel and recognize that it is always the same: it is the idea of a cataclysm, of the breaking in of drunkenly destroying and annihilating powers into a life firm and devoted with all its hopes to values and a conditioned happiness of control. The song achieved, seemingly secure peace and that of life with a laugh sweeping away the faithful structure of art; of mastery and overpowering, of the coming of the strange god, was in the beginning as it was in the middle. And in a later time which enters sympathetically into man's beginnings, we find ourselves in the sign of unity still drawn to that ancient partaking."

IN THE TOILS

"How narrow is the span when we look back upon our own lives; how vast when we contemplate the world's abysmal past! And yet we lose ourselves as easily, as dreamily, in the one as in the other; by virtue of our perception of a unity between the two. As little in the small sphere as in the large can we go back to the time of our birth and the beginning of our days, to say nothing of further back. It lies in darkness before the beginnings of the dawn of consciousness or memory. But with our earliest mental life, when we first enter—as primitive man once entered—into civilization, giving and receiving our first little contributions, we are aware of a sympathy, we feel ourselves recognize that abiding unity; with pleased surprise we acclaim our kinship with the larger whole. And the content of the kinship is always the same: it is the idea of a cataclysm, the invasion of destructive and wanton forces into an ordered scheme and a life bent upon self-control and a happiness conditioned by it. The saga of peace wrung from conflict and seemingly assured; of life laughingly sweeping away the structure of art; of mastery and overpowering, and the coming of the stranger god—all that was there from the beginning, as it was all the way through. And in a late age, which is aware of its affinity with human beginnings, we find ourselves still united with them in that bond of sympathy."

In general there has been little written on the craft of translation. In English the word until well on in the last century meant the scholar's task of rendering the Greek and Latin classics into English. Very often, in English versions of modern works the name of the translator used not to be given. But now there are many translators of modern works of literature by persons in the literary field —I need only mention Mrs. Garnett's and Aylmer Maude's monumental and classic labors on Tolstoi, Scott Moncrieff's English versions of Proust, and many others of the present day. It is practically always a part-time job, an avocation. As a full-time occupation, I hardly think it could earn a living. The pay is poor and grows poorer by reason of the justified improvement in typists' fees, so that the translator must do his own typing or his money payment is small indeed. I have spoken above about the compensations he may hope for.

So now we have arrived at the war period, 1939–45. My husband and I returned to Princeton some six weeks after war broke out, and we spent the costive period until the invasion of the Low Countries partly in the Bahamas and partly in a new house we had built in Princeton. We occupied it until 1946. I look back with nostalgia upon this period, settled as I was in a snug book-lined study, with two fine libraries to draw upon. Where now, I mourn, are my books and notes? These pages are defective, perhaps incorrect, for lack of them. In the midst of war-relief work I found time to translate that irresistible *jeu d'esprit, Die Vertauschten Köpfe,* the inspiration for which had been two poems of Goethe, "The God and the Bayadere" and "Paria"; also *Maia,* a study of Hindu myth and legend by H. Zimmer.

I was able to see a good deal of the Manns, for whom Dr. Abraham Flexner, the first Director of the Institute for Advanced Study, had succeeded in arranging a two-year lectureship in Princeton University. Having these two first-magnitude stars, Mann and Einstein, in his sky, Dr. Flexner once confessed to me his ambition to add Freud to the galaxy; but the great man got no farther than England, where he died some years later. Dr. Mann delivered three lectures, I think, on Faust at this time. I made English versions of them, and he used to come to read the translations to me before he delivered them. One of them, given, I believe, at Swarthmore College, he read to me in June 1940. It is a priceless memory of mine that he began this lecture by saying that he was so shaken by the fall of France that he was unable to put his ideas together, and must apologize for their disconnected character. After reading this sentence he looked quizzically at me and remarked: "Of course that isn't true." Despite our quite genuine emotions, I fear we both chuckled. Dr. Mann speaks very good English, much better than my German, and we correspond each in our native tongue. As a matter of fact I have a poorish gift as a linguist. But at that time

his English lectures impressed me as being in a tongue unknown, which by a stroke of luck I happened to understand.
In these lectures T.M. quoted much Goethe, and I remember
how much I enjoyed putting the delightful simple genial
verse, with its feminine endings, into English. I have been,
only in my own mind of course, conceited enough to fancy
I could make a good new English version of *Faust* Part I!
Of course I have not the necessary scholarship! I must,
here, I feel, confess with shame that I sometimes do not
"really understand" T. Mann until I have undressed his
thought and put English garb on it.

Another memory of that Princeton year comes back to
me: I spent an afternoon with the Manns reading to them
an account of a performance in Oxford (a number of
years ago) of the *Urfaust,* by a company of young German
actors. The name of Arndt, who gave an interesting
interpretation of Mephistopheles, may still be known. The
Faustus, whose own name I have forgotten, a too-sincere
young German with a hard cold, stopped in our house. We
were kept busy making hot lemonades for him. I did not
care for his performance, but neither, really, was I sympathetically affected by the piece itself, and I remember how
shocked they were when I said so. It was with a certain
shock that I myself realized how Marxian my thinking was
at that time. Or was it my Puritan ethics? I mean that I
referred the piece to the class and economic structure of
society. Of course, Proudhon would not be born for more
than a quarter of a century yet; Robert Owen was an
infant when it was written.

What rubbed me the wrong way was that Goethe
seemed nowhere to admit that the dice were loaded in
Faust's favor as against Gretchen. He had not, here, a

strong sense of human values. Perhaps, in his time, he could not have. Who had? I thought of Shakespeare and began going over the plays in my mind. It seems to be a fact, though perhaps it is not a significant one, that the Faust-Gretchen situation does not occur anywhere in his long list of plays. Claudio in *Measure for Measure* is eager to marry Juliet. Angelo deserts Mariana in the same play, but Shakespeare pays him out. Proteus (*The Two Gentlemen of Verona*) forsakes Julia, but she pursues him in the lovely garnish of a boy and Shakespeare brings him back repentant—though clumsily—to her feet. Throughout the plays the classes are mostly kept in water-tight compartments and no such situations as Goethe's favorite one seem to arise. A somewhat similar one occurs in *All's Well;* however, punishment is duly meted out to that ineffable cad, Bertram, Count of Rousillon. I wondered why this was the case. But really, it is not hard to see. Or at least so it seemed to me. Shakespeare—at least the age he lived in—found women more *human* than Goethe's did. There is scarcely a female in the big gallery of Shakespeare's women who *could* have been deserted. They are all too much *Mensch*. Of course, they are practically all high-born. Yet Florizel intended to marry Perdita.

I do not know enough to make anything of these ideas. Perhaps they have been worked up already. The only point I am making is that age for age, class for class, genius for genius, Goethe's ideals were not so loftily human after all.

Maybe these are cynical and destructive thoughts. But really, are we not getting to a point where we have got to test human values on something like these lines? Or else what will become of them in art?

I read the above comments aloud to the Manns one day

in their Princeton house. Frau Dr. was rather shocked,
T.M. non-committal. The two sons agreed with me. All this
from memory, many years ago it was. But Dr. Mann had
already committed himself. In his essay entitled "Goethe
as Representative of the Bourgeois Age," on page 79 of
Essays of Three Decades, American edition, there stand
the sentences:

"In Gretchen's tragic fate, in the guilt of Faust, not a
paragraph, not a social attitude, not an institution is
attacked; here a poet merely discourses with the Eternal
upon man's tragic lot. And so this same poet, as member of
the Weimar Council of State, could sign the death-warrant
of a young girl guilty of child-murder. He signed his name
under the names of the other unpitying ministers, though
the Duke himself would have shown her mercy. 'Ich auch,'
he wrote. I am not the first to find the fact almost as
shattering as the whole of Faust."

The Manns remained only two years in Princeton, in
1939 removing to California, where they built a large
house, living in it until 1952. The family had, some time
before, acquired American citizenship. At this time his
prodigious vitality produced not only *Doctor Faustus* but
also *The Tables of the Law* and *The Holy Sinner.* During
the war he wrote essays and made broadcasts to Germany,
which have been translated by various hands and published under the title *Listen, Germany.* The *Faustus* had so
powerful an impact upon my mind and emotions, it so
depressed my spirits, that I was obliged to "get it off my
chest" by writing a long analysis of it.

The task of rendering the *Faustus* in English was a very
difficult one. I was incompetent to make anything satisfactory of the great musical erudition displayed by the author

207

and was obliged to get help from a competent musicologist, Mosco Carner, now with the BBC. I took a gramophone and records of the Beethoven sonata Opus 111 on my summer holiday in Maine and played it over and over —but of course I am still extremely dissatisfied with my version of the words which Dr. Mann sets to the second movement of the sonata.

I am somewhat hesitant to comment on the circumstances which caused Dr. Mann and his wife to leave the U.S.A. and take up residence in Switzerland, putting up his California home for sale. A recorded broadcast on the BBC two years ago is a forthright statement in which he says that he, no Communist, refuses to "take the anti-Communist shilling." He is, however, still a U.S. citizen. A series of episodes has, I should guess, made American residence distasteful to him, as it has to a fair number of Europeans who once sought and found in it a refuge from persecution. Such people are mostly private individuals; their discomfort is no less keen for being largely subjective. I think it reminds them of their flight from Europe, in the dread decade of the thirties. Now there is nowhere else to go!

I heard that a publishing house in West Berlin plans to issue complete editions of the works of famous prewar authors, such as Hauptmann, Hesse, George, Mann, and others. I know of no plan to publish the collected translations of Dr. Mann's works, comprising all the novels, short stories and *Novellen,* essays, lectures, even a single play. And indeed the indefatigable brain continues to create, being now engaged on a long novel which (I hear) is growing to inordinate length from two fragments published years ago: "Felix Krull." On account of age and other infirmities I have reluctantly abandoned my task of English translator to the great creator. One such infirmity has been the weak craving, while this machine is still to me, to put down, at last, feebly, something of my own creation. I wrote in this sense to T. Mann protesting my debts to him in technique, and in a really touching letter he handsomely admitted that he could not but understand and agree. I treasure this letter, for to most of the reading public, once a translator always a translator.

INDEX

i

A NOTE ON THE TYPE

The text of this book was set on the Linotype in a new face called PRIMER, designed by RUDOLPH RUZICKA, earlier responsible for the design of Fairfield and Fairfield Medium, Linotype faces whose virtues have for some time now been accorded wide recognition.

The complete range of sizes of Primer was first made available in 1954, although the pilot size of 12 point was ready as early as 1951. The design of the face makes general reference to Linotype Century (long a serviceable type, totally lacking in manner or frills of any kind) but brilliantly corrects the characterless quality of that face.

*This book was composed, printed, and bound
by Kingsport Press, Inc., Kingsport, Tenn.*

Typography and Binding design by
GEORGE SALTER